Acclaim for T

MRS. DUBOSE ʼs LAST WISH
The Art of Embracing Suffering

"'Although the world is full of suffering, it is full also of the over-coming of it.' This quote, by Helen Keller, perfectly encapsulates the totality of Thomas Fellows' latest book titled "Mrs. Dubose's Wish: The Art of Embracing Suffering... Fellows perfectly guides the reader through how one may use addiction to ease the suffering and how one can change and grow through their suffering." – Jamie Jeans, - *Cass County Citizen's Journal-Sun* (Atlanta, TX)

"The book recommends itself to those willing to think in larger terms that world does not revolve around us. Like the Bible, one needs to read the book more than once to appreciate his insights and, yes, it is worth more than the $13.95 price. Indeed, the book's profits go to National Institute on Mental Illness." – **William Green,** *Laredo Morning Times* (Laredo, TX)

"Overall, I give "Mrs. Dubose's Last Wish" by Thomas Fellows a 4 out of 5. Fellows brings to light that to having value and worth is not easy. Sometimes society wants the quick and easy way and get no value in return. Once I started reading, I couldn't put it down ... kept me engaged from beginning to end." – **C.A. Hinojosa,** *Mercedes Enterprise* (Mercedes, TX)

"Presented in a manner that is easy top grasp by the reader." – **Jo Anne Embleton,** *Cherokeean Herald* (Rusk, TX)

"Like the Bible, one needs to read the book more than once to ap-preciate his insights and, yes, it is worth more than the $13.95 price. Indeed, the book's profits go to National Institute on Mental Ill-ness." – **Bill Green,** *Laredo Morning Times* (Laredo, TX)

1

"Fellows examines the art of suffering and how human beings need to suffer to develop empathy and a deeper understanding of each other's lives ... Throughout the book, Fellows uses classic literature, history, popular music, movies and the Bible to make his points." – **Sherry Shepard,** *Longview News Journal* **(Longview, TX)**

"'Mrs. Dubose's Last Wish' shares lessons learned by those who have suffered and explains how they are better for it. It is filled with numerous quotes and examples from Scripture, historical figures like Abraham Lincoln, sports legends like Tiger Woods, movie characters like Rocky Balboa from the "Rocky" movies and others." – **Tracy Riggs,** *The Alabama Baptist* **(Birmingham, AL)**

"Usually when someone thinks of a typical self-help book, they think they'll be reading about upbeat emotions such as positivity, energy and self-belief. The last thing most people would think of would be to embrace suffering. That is the focus of Thomas Fellows' book "Mrs. Dubose's Last Wish," a look at how suffering – of any kind – can lead to the strength needed to empathize with fellow humans and enrich one's life, allowing one to gain a greater appreciation for life, love and a closer relationship with God." – **David Bryant,** *Fort Hood Hearld* **(Fort Hood, TX)**

"For regular readers, opening Thomas Fellows' latest book is like running into an old acquaintance ready to share what's been happening in his life. As the title drives home, Fellows pins "The Art of Embracing Suffering" on the example of Mrs. Dubose but he also shares travails and woes he has faced in his life. – **Dean Polling,** *Valdosta Daily Times* **(Valdosta, GA).**

From the Pages of *Mrs. Dubose's Last Wish*

We all suffer from time to time in our lives, some more than others. It's how we react to that suffering that separates the winners from the losers. – **CHAPTER 1**

The strongest predictor of success is the amount of suffering one is willing to embrace. – **CHAPTER 1**

To want to fight after enduring so much pain, you have to not only outlast until the final bell rings, but you also have to overcome trials and tribulations that seem like they will go on forever. – **CHAPTER 1**

When we are on the ground and can't stand up, we tend to think God has forgotten about us. This couldn't be further from the truth because God uses painful experiences not only to build us up, but also others around us. – **CHAPTER 1**

When our complete trust is in God, we have no choice but to thank God for whatever happens, knowing firmly that *He*, and not *we*, has the best handle on our lives. – **CHAPTER 1**

Whatever you are going through at the present time, just know that—believe it or not—God knows what you are going through, and, better yet, he knows what you have to do to get through to the finish line. – **CHAPTER 2**

Whatever you are going through, fear should not have a place in your heart because The Lord is by your side just as a best friend is with you through your worst times, and He is your number one cheerleader during your best times, or, in this digital age, the first one to post your success on social media. He is not afraid to sacrifice for you, even if it means going through a painful, gruesome death on a wooden cross for you. He's already gone through that pain, so that you can have pain no more. – **CHAPTER 2**

When someone tells you that they want you to see something, they're telling you that because they feel as if you have not noticed something that they think would be beneficial for you to see; more than likely, something to make you grow. – **CHAPTER 2**

When I think of someone who is worthy of respect, I immediately think of someone who is hard on themselves. To earn the respect of all, one must be hard on himself. The moment he lets go of this plight, is the moment he begins to lose the respect of many, if not all. – **CHAPTER 3**

I've realized that the most influential don't mind suffering themselves, but if they're even put in a position where they can alleviate another's suffering, they'll do so every single time, often in a hurry. – **CHAPTER 3**

When we love unconditionally—without getting anything back in return—we end up getting just as much back, if not more. The quicker others pain becomes yours is the barometer of how sensitive you are, and, contrary to popular belief, being sensitive is not a sign of weakness, but strength. – **CHAPTER 3**

Suffering isn't easy and *choosing* to suffer is even harder. But in life, we must choose to suffer if we ever want anything accomplished. – **CHAPTER 4**

It is alright for us to pray to God to alleviate our suffering, but only if it furthers his kingdom or will. If you can do that, you know you are on the path to a close relationship with The Lord. – **CHAP-TER 4**

If what you're about to attempt doesn't scare you, what you're attempting to do is not of insignificance. Signs on the highway show significant landmarks such as places to eat, stay, and be entertained. Let what you're striving after show the signs of significance as well. – **CHAPTER 4**

Only when you begin to choose to suffer from time to time do you know your faith is catching on. If you find yourself seeking pleasure all the time instead of pain, check yourself because not only do sacrifice and suffering start with the same letter, they both bring a smile to God. – **CHAPTER 6**

When you're suffering, you naturally think that first and foremost you must dig yourself out of a hole, when in actuality, digging other people out of a hole can prove to be much more effective for alleviating that suffering – **CHAPTER 6**

In many ways we can't choose the fate that God has given us. Some of us are born tall, some of us are born short, some of us white, some of us black. What we can do, however, is react to what God has given us because he has given us free-will. We are not robots programmed by God; we have choices. Whatever problems you are going through, know that in the end, you have a choice as to how you will react to it. – **CHAPTER 6**

Our first inclination is look out for ourselves when we are suffering, and, when we do so, it often causes us to forget to look out for the needs of others. Christ, on the other hand, got hurt on the cross so he could *help* people. He didn't have to do so, but he wanted to make us whole again. – **CHAPTER 6**

Sometimes, the reason God wants us to suffer is to get that big part of us that is off the track back on the rails. He does this because this is the only way we will be able to see what we are doing wrong. Are you wise enough to realize this? I hope so. – **CHAPTER 6**

Life is very reactionary; those who react with the most bravery during the most harrowing times are the ones who are remembered. In debates, politicians, are taught by their debate coaches not to react in a negative way even if their competitors are trying to get under their skin. – **CHAPTER 6**

ALSO BY THOMAS FELLOWS

Forget Self-Help
He Spoke with Authority
The Criminal

TO BE PUBLISHED IN THE FUTURE BY THOMAS FELLOWS

LISTEN UP: SEEK ENOUGH ADVICE, AND, ONE DAY, YOU'LL BE GIVING IT

ALONE AT THE LUNCH TABLE: HOW TO RISE FROM REJECTION

WHEN YOU SEE IT: BELIEF IN UNCERTAINTY

AFTER THE SHAMPOO: CONDITIONED FOR EXCELLENCE

INPUT-OUTPUT: OUR FINAL PRODUCT COMES FROM OUR INITIAL ACTIONS

RELATIVELY SPEAKING: WHEN AND WHEN NOT TO COMPARE YOURSELF TO THE REST

OVERLOOKED: BEING AND FINDING THAT DIAMOND IN THE ROUGH

ROLLING THE DICE: RISK AVERSION EXPLAINED

CONSTANT ENABLING: CREATING AN ATMOSPHERE OF PERMANENT CHANGE

SETTING PROPER EXPECTATIONS: ALLOWING YOURSELF TO GET CAUGHT OFF GUARD LESS

MRS. DUBOSE'S LAST WISH
THE ART OF EMBRACING SUFFERING

THOMAS FELLOWS

Mrs. Dubose's Last Wish

The Art of Embracing Suffering

© 2021 Thomas Fellows

ISBN 978-1-954617-10-0 paperback

978-1-954617-11-7 eBook

Yawn's Publishing
678-880-1922   www.yawnspublishing.com

www.yawnspublishing.com

678-880-1922
Canton, Georgia

Printed in the United States of America

CONTENTS

Introduction

Initially, my fourth book, *When You See It*, was going go be my last book, but after re-reading David Brooks' *The Road to Character*, and thinking I could put what Brooks writes about suffering in conjunction with the suffering that Mrs. Dubose went through in *To Kill a Mockingbird* when she was trying to rid herself of a morphine addiction, I figured I would write a book, this book, *Mrs. Dubose's Last Wish: The Art of Embracing Suffering*, which focused on not only choosing to suffer, but to embrace it. Originally, I was going to float the idea to Brooks for him to write himself[1], but I figured I would save it for myself and see what happens.

In *The Road to Character*, in incredible fashion, Brooks goes on for over three pages in much of his own thoughts describing just what suffering is and how to get through it. When I was going through a lengthy stint of unemployment, which I describe in the book, Brooks words soothed me the way no author had before in my life.

*

The main thesis of this book, I suppose, is that while 99%

---

[1] I have a close connection with Brooks through a fellow student from high school who worked on his book. She took a class of his at Yale and subsequently worked on two of his books after that class.

of the world tries to avoid suffering, the most successful people and people that will be remembered for generations to come, not only *choose* to suffer, but embrace it fully, often asking for more. Suffering is not for the faint of heart, but neither is anything that leads to something truly meaningful.

Through my usual use of literature historical figures, scripture, popular music, and popular movies, and my own personal experiences, I try to not only encourage you, the reader, to choose to suffer as I have said in the paragraph below, but also to embrace it. Malcom Gladwell once said, "good writing does not succeed or fail on the strength of its ability to persuade. It succeeds or fails on the strength of its ability to engage you, to make you think, to give you a glimpse into someone else's head." I hope I achieved this throughout the pages of *Mrs. Dubose's Last Wish*.

Acknowledgments

I want to thank Dr. Ghamei for taking me seriously when I first emailed him.

I want to thank David Brooks for taking me seriously when I met him at his talk at Peachtree Presbyterian Church.

I want to thank Walter Henegar for introducing me to David Brooks' book, *The Road to Character*, in a sermon at Westside Presbyterian Church.

I want to thank Adam Kovarus for being there for me when I had just gotten fired and was suffering.

I want to thank Dr. Bill Clarkson for writing a letter back to me during my first semester at Samford. The Westminster Schools is a better place because of the great job you did there.

I want to thank Russell Lovelady for being there for me during my suffering at The University of Alabama.

I want to thank Dr. Louis Markos for taking me seriously when I asked him to review my second book.

I want to thank Susan Hamm, a classmate of mine at Samford, for giving me the encouragement I needed to start writing these books.

I want to thank Henry Quillian for taking me seriously when I published my first book.

I want to thank all my co-workers at ServerMonkey for giving my life a new start in August. If this book becomes a *New York Times* Bestseller, I'll bring in a 200-count nugget tray from Chick-fil-a.

I want to thank Malcom Gladwell for bringing this out of me. I look forward to hearing your thoughts on my 8th book, *After the Shampoo: Conditioned for Excellence*, which takes your fifth book, *David and Goliath: Underdogs, Misfits, and the Art of Battling Giants*, a step further. The only hint I'll give you is that I focus heavily on the hard determinism in this book and quote Baruch de Spinoza when he once said, "men are deceived because they think themselves free…and the sole reason for thinking so is that they are conscious of their own actions, and ignorant of the causes by which those actions are determined."

I want to thank K.T. Taratus for being there through both the good and bad times.

I want to thank my father, Hank Fellows, for teaching me to take people seriously.

Lastly, none of these books would have happened, my sales career wouldn't have finally flourished the way it has, and I wouldn't be working on an academic case study with a Texas congresswoman to change how America looks at education had it not been for the excellent parenting of my mother, Pam Neal Fellows. When I was four years-old, we were at Ace Hardware on Roswell Road in Atlanta. I saw some green army men that I wanted that were $4. I asked her for them. The majority of parents would have told their kid "no" not to spoil them or told their kid yes and spoiled them. Instead of doing either, my mother decided to empower me. It was

16

fall and she said that if I raked four bags of leaves at $1 dollar each, I could earn $4 and purchase them myself. This was even more significant considered we grew in Buckhead. I raked those four bags of leaves and the rest is history. George Washington must have had a similar mother to the one that I had; after all, he once said, "My mother was the most beautiful woman I ever saw. All I am I owe to my mother. I attribute my success in life to the moral, intellectual and physical education I received from her."

Foreword

Suffering is a fact of life. And so is joy. The two aspects go together. One could never know what suffering was unless one had experienced joy. And what could joy be unless you knew what it was like not to be joyful? An excess of virtue is a vice. One doesn't exist without the other. All nature is dichotomy, duality, dialectic. You'll find these ideas in Buddha and Emerson and Hegel and elsewhere. They are old but worth recalling.

There is suffering in life. So what does it mean to embrace it, as Thomas Fellows recommends? I would suggest that there is a positive embracing and a negative one. The positive embrace is spiritual, in a sense; it makes you whole, larger, better. The negative embrace is masochistic; it breaks you up, makes you smaller, worse.

The positive embrace of suffering is the balance between denial and masochism. It involves accepting a reality: something bad has happened, an illness, an injury, a harm. After the negative event has occurred, there is no point bemoaning that it has happened. A negative attitude towards a negative event doesn't produce anything positive. You should worry about something harmful before it happens, when you can do something to prevent or mitigate it. After it has happened, there's no point to worry. Then, it's the time for acceptance, and repair. Worry beforehand; fix afterwards. Most people do the reverse. They don't worry enough beforehand; and because they worry so much afterwards, they can't fix anything.

So we accept suffering beginning with the fact that something harmful has happened, and we can't change that it has happened. We accept it. Now the question is what to do with it. We are in pain; the first reaction can be to reduce the pain. There's no harm in that reaction. Some reduction in pain might help us think more clearly, or decide what to do about the illness or injury or harm. But if we focus only on reducing the pain, and nothing else, then nothing really changes except our false mental state of pain-reduction. We might take the path of drugs, the most common path; for some reason nature or God put opiate receptors in the brain, and planted opium poppies in the land, and the two things match up like a lock and key to destroy those who enjoy the effect too much. Pain reduction is a means, and not an end; if it becomes an end, it is the end.

After some reduction in pain, we can turn to understanding why the harmful event happened. We seek an explanation. Maybe we had a role; maybe we could have done something different. Usually there is at least something that could have been changed, even if minor. We can learn from that realization, not for this harm, which has happened and can't be changed, but for future harms, which we might prevent with our new-found knowledge. Mistakes happen; there's no avoiding them; their purpose should be to learn from them, so that future mistakes don't happen, or happen less. If we don't learn, then the mistakes mean nothing; they will be repeated forever.

Failure is the prelude to success, if mistakes lead to learning. But if no learning happens, then failure simply leads to more failure, and a downward denouement.

So we reduce pain; we learn from the harmful event; and then we try to mitigate it. Perhaps its worst outcomes can be delayed or diminished in some way; perhaps we can get out of it more clearly in some manner. We look for ways out. We find our way out.

Sometimes it doesn't work this way. Sometimes there is no reason at all why something happened to us, so we can't learn from it. Sometimes there's no mitigation, and no way out. Sometimes it's just a terrible calamity, with no why or wherefore and no exit. Thankfully, such terrible experiences, though present in human life, are uncommon. They do happen, and when they do, all one can do is to turn inward in one's silence, and outward to the silence of the universe, and ask for compassion.

But for the vast majority of harms in human existence, there are some whys, wherefores, and exits. And when it's over, when we come out of it, when the worst is behind us, that's when we can harvest the greatest product of our pain: empathy. Here's a word that didn't exist in human history until the early 1900s, created by a German psychologist: *Einfuhlung* – feeling into. A few years later, the concept was translated into English using Greek roots: "em" into, "pathos" feeling – empathy. Pathos means feeling in Greek but it also implies pain. If you don't have pain, you can't have empathy, you can't feel into the pain of another. The term *sympathy* existed previously, meaning "with" (sym) pathos. You are there *with* the feeling of pain. But empathy takes it further: you are *in* the feeling of pain.

When you emerge from the pain of your harmful experience, you can then see the pain of others, and not only be with them, but get into the pain, feel it for yourself, know that you've felt it. And then you can get out of yourself, and put yourself in their place, and see how it feels for them. This process of getting out of yourself is a spiritual tendency; it's the basis for a larger awareness of life and the universe. And it has important personal and social consequences. It ends your own selfishness, and makes a you a friend to another. It makes you able to love, and help, and feel the joy of relationship. And it diminishes conflict between classes of society, and races, and religions, and nations. It's the basis of a nonviolent attitude toward life, a way to end injustice without harming the unjust. This approach requires the willingness to accept suffering instead of inflicting it. And of course, only one who has suffered, and learned how to accept, tolerate and rise above it, is capable of such nonviolent living. Most humans have not reached this mental state. Most don't even know what it means.

- **Dr. Nassir Ghaemi,** *New York Times* **Best Selling Author of** *A First -Rate Madness: Uncovering the Links Between Mental Illness and Leadership*

"It's amazing the way things, apparently disconnected, hang together." – Charlie, *Flowers for Algernon*. Daniel Keyes

"So, Verily, With Every Difficulty, There is Relief" – Quaran 94:5

"In virtually any other serious sickness, a patient who felt similar devastation would be lying flat in bed, possibly sedated and hooked up to the tubes and wires of life support systems … His individualism would be necessary, unquestioned, and honorably attained. However, the sufferer of depression has no such option." - William Styron, *Darkness Visible*

"I brought this out in him, his toughness. I would do all kind of things to mess him up, usually on the golf course. Man, did he get angry with me. He could say one word, and that one word was the release word that the whole training was over. I said "Tiger, if you never utter that word, I promise you that you'll never meet another person as mentally tough as you." – Earl Woods, father of Tiger Woods

"He played mind games on me on almost every shot I hit until I grew up until I accepted it, and then it was nothing." – Tiger Woods

"Let me not beg for the stilling of my pain but for the heart to conquer it." Rabindranath Tagore (Indian Hindu mystic philosopher)

"Only within our body, with its Heart and mind, can bondage and suffering be found, and only here can we find true liberation." - Guatama Buddha

"As I writer, you get to say what you think." – What David Brooks said when he met me on April 25th, 2019 at Peachtree Presbyterian Church in Atlanta, GA. I was 29-years-old at the time. That was exactly what I needed to hear.

To: Freddy

"We delight in the beauty of the butterfly, but rarely admit the changes it has gone through to achieve that beauty." - Maya Angelou

1

When Do I Fight Again?

I've interviewed a lot in my seven-year career in software sales. As you can imagine, if you know me or read my books, the one who is interviewing me is often left with the sense that they've never quite interviewed someone like me before—whether that be put in a positive or negative sense. Sometimes I'll quote John Wooden[2] or ask a question that is really quite deep for an interview for a software sales position. My favorite question to ask the interviewer is: "considering that if I get the job, the odds of me suffering during it at some point are quite great, can you name a time during your career where you've suffered and tell me about it so *when* I suffer during the job, I know you'll be able to help me."

Much of the time, the person interviewing me is impressed by the question; when that happens, I know that this is a person whom I would want to work for. We all suffer from time to time in our lives, some more than others. It's how we react to that suffering that separates the winners from the losers.

---

[2] John Wooden is code for me really quoting myself.

No Rainy Days

In two of my favorite sports commercials of all time, Tiger Woods, tells the viewer how he has become one of the best golfers. It wasn't through playing in seventy-five-degree weather, but it was through hitting golf ball after golf ball on rainy days. In the first commercial, he says, "I don't have to lift weights, I don't have to rebuild my swing, I don't have to practice at night, unless I want to beat Tiger Woods." In the second commercial, he says, "A rainy day is my chance to be at home, be a fan, be a kid, be lazy, problem is, there are no rainy days."

The strongest predictor of success is the amount of suffering one is willing to embrace. When I spoke at my Alma mater, Samford University, I told the business students that, "to get to do what you really want to do, you're going to have to do things you don't really want to do." It's true; when I was wrote my first book, *Forget Self-Help*, the most tedious part of the job was editing the book. If one was to buy the first edition, he/she could probably tell I didn't like to do it as there were a lot of typos and mistakes in there.

No one forced Tiger Woods to become as great as he has become; only he did that. I grew up adoring Tiger Woods[3], starting in 1997 when he won the Masters just like everyone who was a junior golfer did. I actually brought in, once or twice, a Tiger Woods

---

[3] One of the first biographies I ever read was *On the Course with Tiger Woods* by Matt Christopher in the late 1990's.

American Express ad to my History class in 10th grade at Westminster when I took a class from Mr. Tribble for the first time. He had me read the ad aloud to the class. When Tiger had his off the course problems, I was disappointed in him, but still, was eager to see him come back. Through Tiger's suffering from his injuries[4], however, people noticed that he has become a better human being. In "Golf: How Tiger Woods finally managed to change stripes," Michael Donaldson wrote that his former caddie, Steve Williams, remarked that he didn't recognize Tiger Woods at the most recent Masters in the spring of 2019. Furthermore, Rickie Fowler[5] commented "He's a different Tiger. He's freed up so much. His guard is down, he's a lot more open, friendly. Before, in his prime, it was very much tunnel vision. He went out and did his job and took care of business. He's a lot more engaging now. Freer."

Even Charley Hoffman, another professional golfer, quipped, "He's a better person now. He's more humble, more personable. He has learned from his mistake and come out stronger and better."

The Tiger Woods that I respect the most is one who, even though he could have easily won the par 3 tournament at the Masters, would intentionally try to lose the tournament because no person had ever won the par 3 tournament and the actual Masters tournament in the same year. Tiger, more than any other golfer, respected the traditions and the aura of the game of golf, and because

---

[4] Complete list of Tiger's injuries in Appendix A.
[5] I actually remember seeing Rickie Fowler's name atop the Junior Golf Scoreboard rankings when I was a ranked golfer myself; obviously, I was ranked much lower.

so, he became one of the top three golfers of all time.[6]

Speaking of golf and getting back to suffering, one moment I will never forget while I was growing up playing junior golf was when I was at Georgia Tech Golf Camp in Rome, GA, at Stone Bridge Golf Club. During the day-time, we would go around to different stations including putting, long game, chipping, and finally, sand bunkers. To an average golfer, bunkers are one of the most menacing obstacles one has to encounter. To a seasoned pro, when they have a good lie in the bunker, they would actually rather be in a bunker rather than long rough.

I still haven't forgotten about what one of my counselors said about how to react when you found that your ball went into a bunker. He said rather than being alarmed, he wanted us to *smile*. It's eerily similar to what James Oglethorpe, founder of the state of Georgia, would say 250 years earlier when he dealt with many problems including political unrest and residents fighting with one another. Even though Oglethorpe faced many troubles, he seemed to smile during them, remarking sarcastically to a Fellow Trustee, "I am here in one of the most delightful Situations as man could be, a great number of Debts, empty Magazine [,] no money to supply them, Numbers of People to be fed, mutinous Soldiers to Command, a Spanish Claim & a large body of Their troops not far from us. But ... these Difficulties rather animate me than daunt me."

Just think, what if you smiled at every bunker you got in?

---

[6] In no particular order, in my very humble opinion, I think the three best golfers of all time are Jack Nicklaus, Tiger Woods, and Bobby Jones.

What if you thanked God for the challenging moments you got to attack? I've said this in one of my previous books, but Bill McDermott[7] always encouraged me to embrace the journey, rather than the destination. Was it enjoyable to have an academic at a Christian writers conference treat me as if I were nothing when I asked if he was interested in my first book? No, but it made it that much more special when one of my favorite authors of all time, Nassir Ghaemi, *New York Times* best-selling author of *First -Rate Madness*, requested to meet with me while he was in Atlanta.

I've used this quote by Robert E. Lee in my previous books, and I'll use it again right now: "Sad thoughts", Lee observed, "will sometimes come over us.... They are the shadows to our picture. They bring out prominently the light & bright spots. They must not cover up all. They must not hide the picture itself." Use the shadows, Lee advised, "as a medium through which to view life correctly." Ironically, that quote comforted an African-American I know who works at a restaurant I frequent often. She was very depressed, and when I told her the quote, it comforted her a great deal.

It's interesting to note that however much we suffer or however low we get, Isaiah 43:2 tells us, "When you pass through the waters, I will be with you; and when you pass through the rivers,

---

[7] Bill McDermott is present day CEO of ServiceNow after spending 16 years as CEO of SAP. You probably haven't heard of ServiceNow because it is a B2B (Business to Business) vs. a B2B (Business to Consumer) company, but in McDermott's first full year with the company, it zoomed up 133 spots in the Fortune 100 rankings from 703 to 570. It was also recently ranked #1 in the Future 50 by Fortune.

they will not sweep over you. When you walk through the fire, you will not be burned; the flames will not set you ablaze." What comfort is it knowing that the God of the universe who created us is with us through all of our struggles, no matter how hard they get? Once we know that, we have the strength to do anything, no matter how hard the struggle may seem.

*

In *Rocky*, the moment the movie starts, you know that the theme of the movie is the exact same theme of this book: embracing constant struggle. In the opening scene, there are hard punches, blood, sweat, and lastly, the yelling of fans encouraging the fighters to keep going. Merriam Webster defines a *fighter* as someone who does not give up. As we examine the movie throughout this book, we will see the reason that Rocky (Slyvester Stallone) is ultimately victorious is that he refuses to give up, no matter what happens to him. After the fight, which Rocky wins, he goes into the locker room, where the viewer is first introduced to Rocky's nickname: "The Italian Stallion." I'm not sure what it is about the nickname, but it elicits trust and respect; in other words, someone you don't want to mess with. After the official for the fight hands out the earnings for both Rocky and his opponent, "Spider," Rocky has only one thing to ask: "When do I fight again?"

To want to fight after enduring so much pain, you have to not only outlast until the final bell rings, you have to overcome trials and tribulations that seem like they will go on forever. In John Mayer's "Bigger than My Body," he speaks to this brave yearning. In the song he admits that he's down and out and has little hope. He still tells the listener that one day he will be on top, that one day, he will be airborne. When we are on the ground and can't stand up, we tend to think God has forgotten about us. This couldn't be further from the truth because God uses painful experiences not only to build us up, but also others around us.

One myth that has been floating around in the "prosperity gospel"[8] circles is that once you become a Christian, you will no longer have trouble, sorrow, or pain in your life. Scripture, however, says that this couldn't be further from the truth. In one of the most powerful books of the Bible, Job, the author describes the pain that Job went through. Here is the summary of the book below from my Zondervan Bible:

> The book of Job is named for its main character, a righteous man who was very rich. Even after losing everything he owned and suffering from a terrible sickness, Job still confessed his love for God.

> The book questions the reasons for suffering, especially the suffering of people who love God are good. Job's friends insisted he was suffering as punishment for his sin. Job defended himself by insisting that he had done nothing seriously wrong and then expressed his trust in God.

> Then God spoke and showed his mighty power. Job finally admitted that God is too great and wonderful for

---

[8] Now that I live in Houston, it only seems fitting that I should have a debate with Joel Osteen on what it means to suffer as a Christian and if the Bible really says that if you're a Christian, you'll automatically be healthier and wealthier.

us to understand.

The thing that strikes me most is the amount of humility and trust that Job showed even when God appeared like he had turned his back on him. It took me such a long time to have the faith in The Lord to realize he knows what's best for me, but slowly but surely, I can feel myself trust Him more and more in my life. One of the most distraught moments in my life was just six months ago. After essentially being unemployed for sixteen months, I felt as if I were finally about to land a good job with a growing tech company. I got along well with my hiring manager, and was sent to the next round with the Head of HR. We were getting along really well when I realized my power was running low on my laptop. I went to go to get the power-cord and plugged it back in to make sure my computer did not go off. We finished the interview, and I anxiously awaited to hear back from the outsourced recruiter to see if I had gotten the job.

When I heard back from her, she revealed the unfortunate news that I did not get the job. When I asked why, she started to chuckle and immediately asked me if I usually work from home. I responded that I did, and while laughing, she told me that the head of HR told her that she saw me in boxers when I went to go get the power cord! She thought it was funny, but I was crushed. I had literally interviewed at dozens of firms in the past year—I was either overqualified or under-qualified for the job—and still had not found work.

Two of my best friends had remarked that you don't need to wear pants in an interview, shorts or boxers would work because the screen only catches your chest up. When I told some people I knew what had happened, I was beyond disappointed and couldn't believe what had happened. It was hard to trust that God knew what was best for me—that he had my back. However, in Job 1:13-22, it reads,

One day when Job's sons and daughters were feasting and drinking wine at the oldest brother's house, a messenger came to Job and said, "The oxen were plowing and the donkeys were grazing nearby, and the Sabeans attacked and made off with them. They put the servants to the sword, and I am the only one who has escaped to tell you!"
While he was still speaking, another messenger came and said, "The fire of God fell from the heavens and burned up the sheep and the servants, and I am the only one who has escaped to tell you!"

While he was still speaking, another messenger came and said, "The Chaldeans formed three raiding parties and swept down on your camels and made off with them. They put the servants to the sword, and I am the only one who has escaped to tell you!"

While he was still speaking, yet another messenger came and said, "Your sons and daughters were feasting and drinking wine at the oldest brother's house, when suddenly a mighty wind swept in from the desert and struck the four corners of the house. It collapsed on them and they are dead, and I am the only one who has escaped to tell you!"

At this, Job got up and tore his robe and shaved his head. Then he fell to the ground in worship and said:

"Naked I came from my mother's womb, and naked I will depart. The Lord gave and the Lord has taken away; may the name of the Lord be praised."

In all this, Job did not sin by charging God with wrong doing.

The most amazing thing to me in this passage is the faith that Job shows in The Lord despite all his pain and suffering. Almost immediately after the pain he goes through, instead of complaining to God for the suffering, he has the wherewithal to *thank* God for the suffering. When our complete trust is in God, we have no choice but to thank God for whatever happens, knowing firmly that *He*, and not *we*, has the best handle on our lives. It's difficult to give up that sense of control, but when give up that sense of direction, we often find we are more in control than we have ever been. When we go to a foreign country, we rely on a tour-guide to tell us which parts of town are good for us and which parts pose a great danger. The Lord Our God is that tour guide for us; he has our best interest in mind.

2

Stand Firm

If any book in modern day history was about courage, *To Kill a Mockingbird,* by Harper Lee, might be the first book that comes to mind. Set in a sleepy old Southern town in the 1930's, a prominent white lawyer in town is charged to defend a black man named Tom Robinson, who was accused of raping a white woman. Possibly the most courageous act in the book is more than likely overlooked by the casual reader. We can learn much from it, which is why the title of the book is named for the person who carries out it out. There is a character named Mrs. Dubose in the book whose chief concern in life—to Scout and Jem at least—seems to revolve around making their life complete hell. Whenever they walk by Mrs. Dubose's house, whatever they say does not seem to be good enough for her; she often yells at the children in complete disgust.

One day, Jem had simply had enough of Mrs. Dubose and her insults. When Mrs. Dubose criticized Atticus for defending Tom Robinson, Jem decided to cut off all of the tops of her camelias in her front yard. When he does this, Atticus and Mrs. Dubose decide his form of punishment will be him reading to her.

She was horrible. Her face was the color of a dirty pillowcase, and the corners of her mouth glistened with wet, which inched like a glacier down the deep grooves enclosing her chin. Old-age liver spots dotted her cheeks, and her pale eyes had black pinpoint pupils. Her hands were knobby, and the cuticles were grown up over her fingernails. Her bottom plate was not in, and her upper lip protruded; from time to time she would draw her nether lip to her upper plate and carry her chin with it. This made the wet move faster.

I didn't look any more than I had to. Jem reopened Ivanhoe and began reading. I tried to keep up with him, but he read too fast. When Jem came to a word he didn't know, he skipped it, but Mrs. Dubose would catch him and make him spell it out. Jem read for perhaps twenty minutes, during which time I looked at the soot-stained mantelpiece, out the window, anywhere to keep from looking at her. As he read along, I noticed that Mrs. Dubose's corrections grew fewer and farther between, that Jem had even left one sentence dangling in mid-air. She was not listening.

I looked toward the bed.

Something had happened to her. She lay on her back, with the quilts up to her chin. Only her head and shoulders were visible. Her head moved slowly from side to side. From time to time she would open her mouth wide, and I could see her tongue undulate faintly. Cords of saliva would collect on her lips; she would draw them in, then open her mouth again. Her mouth seemed to have a private existence of its own. It worked separate and apart from the rest of her, out and in, like a clam hole at low tide. Occasionally it would say, "Pt," like some viscous substance coming to a boil.

When we examine Jem's description of Mrs. Dubose, it is clear that she is suffering mightily, although Jem did not know it at the time. What we understand is the saliva she is producing at an alarming rate is the result of going through a massive morphine withdrawal, which would test the grit of all. After Mrs. Dubose no longer corrects him while reading, what he doesn't understand is that the pain of her suffering had grown too intense for her to even care anymore.

In many ways, when we suffer, to not let the pain affect us any longer is the best way to free ourselves of it. The pain that Mrs. Dubose went through was very similar to the pain that the Israelites went though in Exodus. Exodus 1:11 says,

> So they put slave masters over them to oppress them with forced labor, and they built Pithom and Rameses as store cities for Pharaoh. But the more they were oppressed, the more they multiplied and spread; so the Egyptians came to dreas the Israelites and worked them ruthlessly. They made their lives bitter with hard labor in brick and mortar and all kinds of work in the fields; in all their hard labor the Egyptians used them ruthlessly.

Just as the Egyptians were worked ruthlessly, so, too, was Mrs. Dubose. In "Why Addictions are So Hard to Break," by Jennifer Kunst, she explains how, early on, addiction becomes something that we must all encounter.

Think of it from the point of view of a baby—the point of view that we all have at the base of our personalities. The allure of addiction is that it allows you, in fantasy, to create an artificial mother. You no longer need a real mom to give you milk, comfort, and support. You don't have to do the real hard work of taking in what she gives and using it to grow emotionally. With an addiction, you get to bypass all of that tough human stuff. You don't have to wait. You don't have to suffer. You don't need what mom has to offer because you can make it yourself. You even can give it to yourself. To put it in vivid psychoanalytic terms, you've created a synthetic breast-on-demand.

What Mrs. Dubose seemed to be doing all along was bypassing that "tough human stuff." By taking morphine, she *felt* free, but in actuality she was prisoner of herself. She knew that until she chose to suffer on purpose, she would never become free. In our materialistic, consumeristic society, everyone revolves around *not* suffering. At the movies, we are immediately encouraged to quench our thirst or ease our hunger. Ads for clothes in magazines tell us that we are currently suffering because we don't have the latest style.

If we're constantly encouraged not to suffer, then why did I write a book about *embracing* suffering? The reason is because the times when I have been most joyful, gotten want I wanted, or noticed that I'd grown in my faith with The Lord were because I *embraced* suffering, or, at the very least, learned from it.

In Christina Aguilera's, "Fighter," she says this with more passion than I could say. In the chorus of the song, she does what

I encourage, you, the reader, to do in the previous chapter. She thanks her previous lover for transforming her into a fighter. She realizes she has had to exert more energy through her trials, but she also realizes that because of that, she has become more powerful. Even though we may go through pain, we must remember Psalm 27:1, which tells us "The Lord is my light and my salvation—whom shall I fear? The Lord is my stronghold of life—of whom shall I be afraid?" What's even more encouraging is that God himself came down to this earth in the form of Jesus so that he could go through suffering just like us. What other religion can claim that their deity did just that? I say in chapter 5 of *The Criminal: The Power of an Apology* that "Jesus never seeks earthly might. To be a king is to be rich, powerful, carry a good name, and have lots of servants. I guess Jesus never got the memo. For him, power was in being *with* us, not *over* us."

One of my favorite teachers from high school was a man by the name of Joe Tribble whom I mentioned earlier. He was an incredible cross-country coach. What made him so incredible and gave his teams the ability to win so many state championships was that he did every single work-out with his runners. Because of this, at the actual meet, when Tribble was pushing his runners to keep going, they could listen to him more, because he knew what they were going through at that very moment. Whatever you are going through at the present time, just know that—believe it or not—God knows what you are going through, and, better yet, he knows what you have to do to get through to the finish line.

You can't be afraid of your obstacles because you have The Lord on your side.

Later on, in *To Kill a Mockingbird*, if we look closely, we begin to see why it is that Mrs. Dubose has Jem read in the first place is an interaction that Mrs. Dubose has with Atticus.

> Mrs. Dubose smiled at him. For the life of me I could not figure out how she could bring himself to speak to him when she seemed to hate him so. "Do you know what time it is, Atticus?" she said. "Exactly fourteen minutes past five. The alarm clock's set for five-thirty. I want you to know that.

> It suddenly came to me that each day we had been staying a little longer at Mrs. Dubose's, that the alarm clock went off for a few minutes later every day, and that it was well into one of her fits by the time it sounded. Today she had antagonized Jim for nearly two hours with no intention of having a fit, and I felt hopelessly trapped. The alarm clock was the signal of our release; if one day it did not ring; what would we do?

Mrs. Dubose wanted Atticus to know the progress she was making because she wanted to let him know that she was not going to let him down. To Mrs. Dubose, Atticus served as an accountability partner, one who would encourage as well as challenge. Mrs. Dubose was kicking her habit minute by minute, step by step, which is the approach that anyone must take to kick their habit.

I've had friends in the past struggle with alcoholism. Instead of posting something on social media or telling friends how they were sober for such-in-such weeks, months or years, I encouraged them to tell people, because they were sober for that long, what they've been able to accomplish or what mark they have made on the world because of their sobriety. That way, it wouldn't be so much of a countdown of what they've accomplished, but rather they can be reminded about how much they—and the world—are better off because of their sobriety.

Be Still

When the Israelites fled Pharaoh, they knew it would be a challenge; what they didn't know, however, is how much they would have to suffer to get the Promised Land.

As Pharaoh approached, the Israelites looked up, and there were the Egyptians, marching after them. They were terrified and cried out to The Lord. They said to Moses, "was it because there were no graves in Egypt that you had brought us to the desert to die? What have you done to us by brining us out of Egypt? Didn't we say to you in Egypt, 'leave us alone; let us serve the Egyptians'? It would have been better for us to serve the Egyptians than to die in the desert!"

Moses answered the people, "Do not be afraid. Stand firm and you will see the deliverance the Lord will bring you today. The Egyptians you see today will never see you again. The Lord will fight for you; you only need to be still."

What's remarkable is that when we are suffering, the *last* thing we are told is to be still. What Moses is telling us to do is completely different. He's encouraging his people that to get out of the current tumultuous environment they are now in, they must be still. When a gymnast is about to start his/her routine, or a swimmer is about to start his/her race, in order to have the best routine or race, they need to be still at the start. Without that stillness at the start, it is impossible to be composed, and if one is not composed at the start, how can he/she expect to get through the race/meet?

Before Moses tells the Israelites to be still, they were terrified and cried out to the Lord. They questioned if the Lord had just brought them out to die. Have you ever thought that way when you were suffering?

There is a decent chance that, in the same way the Israelites cried out to God when in the desert, that the men from the colonies were also crying for protection and warmth in the bitter cold when they were crossing the Delaware River. When they were preparing to make the voyage, George Washington knew the words that would carry them to victory were the words below by Thomas Paine:

These are the times that try men's souls. The summer soldier and the sunshine patriot will, in this crisis, shrink from the service of their country; but he that stands by it now, deserves the love and thanks of man and woman.

It's only fitting that Paine uses the verb *stands* because that's exactly the verb that Moses uses in the previous pages. In a classroom, you sit because you are absorbing the information that is being taught by the teacher. Once you're at a graduation ceremony, you have to stand to walk across the stage to get your diploma. You can't walk without standing first. When a politician is being sworn into office, they are not sitting either. Even Abraham Lincoln knew that standing was important, for 85 years later, in Dunkirk, NY, Lincoln would say, "Standing as I do, with my hand upon this staff and under the folds of the American flag, I ask you to stand by me so long as I stand by it."

As the Mountain Air

Later on, in *To Kill a Mockingbird*, when Jem is about to go read again to Mrs. Dubose, Atticus stops him and says, "she's dead, son. She's not suffering any more. She was sick for a long time. Son, didn't you know what her fits were?"

Jem shook his head.

"Mrs. Dubsose was a morphine addict," said Atticus. "She took it as a pain-killer for years. The doctor put her on it, She'd have spent the rest of her life on it and died without so much agony, but she was too contrary—"

"Sir?" said Jem.

Atticus said, "Just before your escapade she called me to make her will. Dr. Reynolds told her she had only a few months left. Her business affairs were in perfect order but she said, "There's still one thing out of order."

"What was that?" Jem was perplexed.

"She said she was going to leave this world beholden to nothing and nobody. Jem, when you're sick as she was, it's all right to make it easier, but it wasn't alright for her. She said she meant to break herself of it before she died, and that's what she did.

Jem said, "You mean that's what her fits were?"

"Yes, that's what they were. Most of the time you were reading to her I doubt if she ever heard a word you said. Her whole mind and body were concentrated on that alarm clock. If you hadn't fallen into your hands, I'd have made you go read to her anyway. It may have been some distraction. There was another reason—"

"Did she die free?" asked Jem.

"As the mountain air" said Atticus.

One of the most interesting words that Atticus uses in the above excerpt is *pain-killer*. Often times, whether we know or not, we ourselves are guilty of taking pain-killers, although they might not be in the form of a pill. In the midst of pain, we might give up going through the struggle we are in, resorting to staying on the sidelines. We might use alcohol, drugs, food, or other substances to block out the suffering. We must remember some other words spoken by Thomas Paine when he said,

The harder the conflict, the more glorious the triumph. What we obtain too cheap, we esteem too lightly; it is dearness only that gives everything its value. I love the man that can smile in trouble, that can gather strength from distress and grow brave by reflection. 'Tis the business of little minds to shrink; but he whose heart is firm, and whose conscience approves his conduct, will pursue his principles unto death.

I suspect you've heard this before, but anything worthwhile in life does not come easy. When Paine talks about smiling in trouble, it reminds me of Chapter 1, when my Georgia Tech golf camp coach told us to smile when we ended up in a bunker. It's counterintuitive, but I feel like the best are thankful for the pain—thankful for the challenge.

Later, Atticus speaks to the fact that Mrs. Dubose could have died without much agony; in other words, she *chose* the pain and misery. That's why Atticus later calls her "the bravest person I ever knew." Bravery is most respected when times are tough, when the tough not only get going, but they are present in the suffering, because they know—as well as in the case of Mrs. Dubose—that they will eventually be free. If they do not get going, as Mrs. Dubose did, they will be a prisoner in chains forever.

This was no truer the case than when Washington crossed the Delaware River that cold December night. Washington thought that they would cross the river by midnight, but it wasn't until four the next morning that his army would make it across. Where is your faith in The Lord when you are faced with trouble like this? For me, I struggle to trust in The Lord; I struggle to know that he still knows what is best for me. One verse that you may want to remember is Isaiah 41:10: "Fear not for I am with you. Do not be afraid for I am your God. I will strengthen you, I will help you. I will uphold you with my victorious right hand."

Whatever you are going through, fear should not have a

place in your heart because The Lord is by your side just as a best friend is with you through your worst times and is your number one cheerleader during your best times, or, in this digital age, the first one to post your success on social media. He is not afraid to sacrifice for you, even if it means going through a painful, gruesome death on a wooden cross for you. He's already gone through that pain, so you have pain no more.

See Something

When someone tells you that they want you to see something, they're telling you that because they feel as if you have not noticed something that they think would be beneficial for you to see; more than likely, something to make you grow. This is exactly why Atticus tells Jem "I wanted you to see something about her—I wanted you to see what real courage is, instead of getting the idea what real courage is, instead of getting the idea that courage is a man with a gun in his hand. It's when you know you're licked before you begin but you begin anyway and see it through no matter what. You rarely win, but sometimes you do. Mrs. Dubose won, all ninety-eight pounds of her. According to her views, she died beholden to nothing and nobody. She was the bravest person I ever knew."

For me, the bravest person I have ever known is hands down, without a doubt, my Uncle Walter. Even when I was of a young age, I noticed that something wasn't quite right about his health. As I grew older, I learned that he had a debilitating disease called Multiple Sclerosis or MS for short. According to the mayoclinic.org, "MS, the immune system attacks the protective sheath (myelin) that covers nerve fibers and causes communication problems between your brain and the rest of your body. Eventually, the disease can cause permanent damage or deterioration of the nerves." Uncle Walter has not been able to walk properly in quite some time, ever since I was a young child. Getting outside his apartment is quite a chore, but once a day he does it with the help of crutches, mainly so he doesn't regress anymore.

In many ways, he has suffered like Mrs. Dubose. There was a time a few months ago, however, I completely forgot that he was going through intense pain on a daily basis. It's quite understandable that I forgot that he went through this pain for one simple reason: he never complains; instead, he trudges forward each day like he has nothing to lose and everything to gain. He'll never walk again; we never did get to play that one round of golf together.

With all that being said, if I ever have a son, I know who I'm going to name him after. My sister, Susie, sets up a team to walk in an MS Walk in honor of him. I wrote an email to the family which had these words below:

> Here's to a man who has fought with bravery to which none of us know, to a man who truly understands that to love someone, you have to sacrifice, and, looking to the future, if I am ever fortunate to have a son of my own, he will bear his name-sake. The reason for naming him after Uncle Walter is a no-brainier; I want a son who will fight when others are busy complaining, will look within himself and at not what the world owes him, but what he owes the world, and, most of all, lives out the words of Dave Matthews when he sings, "love is not a whisper; no, love is

strong."

And, without hesitation, if you look at my email signature, he is something I have that I can respect.

"It really is a comfort, in this world, to have anything one can respect." - St. Clare, *Uncle Tom's Cabin*

When I think of someone who is worth of thy respect, I immediately think of someone who is hard on themselves. To earn the respect of all, one must be hard on himself. The moment he lets go of this plight is the moment he begins to lose the respect of many, if not all.

Plight, in case you didn't know, is defined as a "dangerous, difficult, or otherwise unfortunate situation." Why would anyone *choose* to put themselves in that situation? To make themselves free, or as Atticus said, "free as the mountain air."

3

No Such Thing as Neutrality

Martin Luther King Jr. once said, "time itself is neutral; it can be used either destructively or constructively." I would not only agree with him there, but I would also add that in our relationships with others, we are more than likely not bringing a tone of neutrality to the relationship, but we are either bringing joy into their life or taking it away; in other words, we are adding to the pain that they are already going through or taking it away and replacing it with joy in their life.

If there has been any character in the Bible who has played the part of persecutor and encourager, it is Paul. Paul's name wasn't always Paul, though; it used to be Saul. Acts 8:1-3 says, "And Saul was there, giving approval to his (Stephen's) death. On that day a great persecutor broke out against the church at Jerusalem, and all the apostles were scattered throughout Judea and Samaria. Godly men buried Stephen and mourned deeply for him. But Saul began to destroy the church. Going from house to house, he dragged off men and women and put them into prison." When we think of the word great, we naturally think of something positive, but when the word great is put next to a negative noun—as it is about with per-secutor—the word becomes even more menacing.

Speaking of persecution, in the *Lord of the Flies*, by William Golding, there is a character named Piggy who constantly gets persecuted. He is pale and fat, which is how he got his nickname. From the opening pages of the book, you know he is going to get bullied often. When he and Ralph decide to have a meeting, he knows that he will have to reveal his name:

"I don't care what they call me," he said confidentially, "so long as they don't call me what they used to call me at school."

Ralph was faintly interested.

"What was that?"

The fat boy glanced over his shoulder, then leaned toward Ralph.

"They used to call me "Piggy.""

Ralph shrieked with laughter. He jumped up.

"Piggy! Piggy!"

"Ralph—please!"

Piggy clasped his hands in apprehension.

"I said I didn't want—"

"Piggy! Piggy!"

Ralph danced out into the hot air of the beach and then returned as a fighter-plane, with wings swept back, and machine-gunned Piggy.

"Sche-aa-ow!"

He dived in the sand at Piggy's feet and lay there laughing.

"Piggy!"

Piggy grinned reluctantly, pleased despite himself at this much recognition.

"So long as you don't tell the others—"

Ralph giggled into the sand. The expression of pain and concentration returned to Piggy's face.

My point in telling all of you this is that the others on the island, especially Ralph, are obviously bringing pain to Piggy, so much so that he has a rough time surviving. If we take the words that Golding uses—apprehension, pain, and concentration—we can see those are the words that are all a part of suffering in consecutive order. We'll examine those words at the end of the next chapter, but for now let's look at an example where Abraham Lincoln goes out of his way to ease the suffering of little kittens.

I've realized that the most influential don't mind suffering themselves, but if they're even put in a position where they can alleviate another's suffering, they'll do so every single time, often in a hurry. While in the telegraph hut during in a trip to City Point, where Lincoln and his family were invited to Grant's Headquarters, in the spring of 1865 three weeks prior to his assassination, Lincoln saw three stray kittens. Since they seemed to have no one to care for them, Lincoln asked, "where is your mother?" Someone quickly informed him, "the mother is dead." He petted the kitten and said, "then she can't grieve as many a poor mother is grieving for a son lost in battle." Later, he told them, "Kitties, thank God you are cats, and can't understand this terrible strife that is going on. Poor little creatures, don't cry; you'll be taken good care of." He then told a Colonel nearby, "Colonel, I hope you will see that these poor little motherless waifs are given plenty of milk and treated kindly." Watching the whole thing unfold, Colonel Horace Porter, who was the personal secretary to Grant during the war, remarked that it was certainly a spectacle "at an army headquarters, upon the eve of a great military crisis in the nation's history, to see the hand which had affixed the signature to the Emancipation Proclamation and had signed the commissions....from the general-in-chief to the lowest lieutenant, tenderly caressing three stray kittens."

The most important word to me in the whole entire story is *stray*. Stray basically means lost—without a place to call home. But even stray people have had monumental impacts on the world because someone took pity on them and helped out. When Jesus Christ was born, one could say he was a bit of a stray; after all, that first night there was no room for him in the inn; he slept in a manger. Both Joseph and Mary couldn't believe what they had created. In Luke 2:33-35, it reads:

The child's father and mother marveled at what was said about him. Then Simeon blessed them and said to Mary, his mother: "This child is destined to cause the falling and rising of many in Israel, and to be a sign that will be spoken against, so that the thoughts of many hearts will be revealed. And a sword will pierce your own soul too."

At no other point in life was I more stray than when I showed up at Samford in the cold month of January in 2009. After my manic episode in August of 2008, I had been in rehab and worked at Peachtree Golf Club for the remainder of the year. I visited Samford University in Birmingham, AL and decided I would go there. Samford has a mini semester called Jan Term, so I decided it would be best to take a non-academic class to start out, so I took PE. I missed my friends from back home and knew hardly a soul there.

I forget how it all happened, but one day I sat at a table with a bunch of preppy white kids who appeared to be in the fraternity. I started sitting with them at lunch and began to get to know them pretty well. I was a bit nervous that they would ask why I came in the middle of the year, but those questions luckily didn't come up much. The next thing I knew, one of them asked me if I wanted to come to their beach condo in Seaside, FL.

We listened to a lot of Dave Matthews on the way down there (at my request) and ended up having a pretty fun time. I knew how it felt to be a stray in need of milk. Like Lincoln was there for the kittens, my friends from Sigma Chi and other girls were there for me. Sometimes, all you need is a little push to get going, and once you're going, it's impossible to stop. I was a stray no longer.

*

As good a person as I make myself out to be in these books, there was one moment in particular in my life that would make you, the reader, think otherwise. For Chemistry, I had a teacher in 10th grade, Mrs. Sconzo. She was notoriously one of the hardest teachers at the school.[9] She usually only taught AP and Honors classes, except this year the school decided to let her teach regular students. Lucky me.

First semester, her class was hard (I had a 78), but during my second semester, things got even more difficult. There was actually a test where I filled out the whole thing and still got a zero. This was the class that made my parents ask if Westminster was the

---

[9] She literally wrote AP tests on the side.

right school for me. One day after class, during extra help, Mrs. Sconzo and I went into an empty class and decided to have a quick chat. My message to her was that she was a bad teacher. I made my assertion crystal clear. Later, either that year or in the years since, we met up, and she told me I made her literally cry to her husband.

When I came back on the campus in my early career, she was the first teacher that I visited because I wanted to thank her for what a monumental impact she had on my life and tell the students to be thankful for her, despite how hard she was. I passed the class on the dot with a 70, and she still insists that I passed it on my own merit, meaning she did not give me the grade. I suppose in the end, we inflicted pain on each other; I'm thankful for the pain she inflicted on me.[10]

In the movie *Richard Jewell*, another person who was used to getting pain inflicted on himself was the man whom the movie is named for: Richard Jewell. The movie, set in Atlanta when the Olympics came into town in 1996, describes how Jewell was falsely accused of being the one to bomb Centennial Park. The movie revolves—among other things—around the relationship between Jewell and his lawyer, Watson Bryant.[11] Bryant got to know Jewell because he was his mail attendant while Bryant worked at the office of the small business bureau of Georgia. When the FBI investigates Jewell, he makes several mistakes, and, in tense sparring, Jewell asks

---

[10] Despite how poor of a student I was, I still remembered from her class that Gold on the Periodic Table was AU-79, one of the chapter titles in *He Spoke With Authority*.

[11] Watston Bryant's niece in real life was in my class at Westminster.

Bryant why he took his case in the first place, insinuating that he only took it for money and fame. Quick on his feet, Bryant fights back, and asks why out of the thousands of lawyers in Atlanta he called him. In my opinion, the answer is the most pivotal part of the movie, because it highlights the pain that Bryant took away from him: "I picked you because you were the only one at the US Small Business Admin Bureau who didn't treat me like a five-year-old and call me, "bag of snacks" and "blimp," "Michelin Man" and "Pillsbury Doughboy." You're the only one who treated me like a human being!"

Whether we have higher status, or even enemies, we must always treat the other party like a human being. Two times that come to mind are when Lincoln said, "We are not enemies, but friends. We must not be enemies. Though passion may have strained, it must not break our bonds of affection. The mystic chords of memory will swell when again touched, as surely they will be, by the better angels of our nature."

If any relationship was ever strained, it was the relationship between Richard Nixon and John F. Kennedy. Despite this strain, in a pivotal moment, after the Bay of Pigs, Richard Nixon made many phone calls, trying to get the Republicans to help Kennedy. Instead of rubbing the mess in the face of Kennedy, which is what me we might see today in our partisan politics, Nixon simply said, "I saw a man crushed today. He needs our help. I told him to go upstairs and have a drink with his wife." This is how a democracy should work, with one party helping out another; we must have the same goal in mind: the pursuit of excellence.

*

Like I said in the beginning, it's very hard to have a neutral effect on another person; you're either going to cause another pain or take away pain. What's so interesting about Rocky in the movie *Rocky* is that as much pain as he inflicts on himself—such as when he is beating raw meat in the meat house, or running across Philadelphia—he cannot stand to see another person go through pain themselves. The first time you notice this in the movie is when he is walking into a bar. He sees a bum outside the bar who appears to be passed out, drunk. Rocky literally picks him up and promptly drops him in a booth to rest. It's almost as if helping someone up is part of Rocky's routine.

Later, we see another time where Rocky is benevolent: he refuses to break the thumbs of someone who needs to pay a loan back. When the man offers to give him his coat, he says "don't bother." When we love unconditionally—without getting anything back in return—we end up getting just as much back, if not more. The quicker others pain becomes yours is the barometer of how sensitive you are, and, contrary to popular belief, being sensitive is not a sign of weakness, but strength.

In another story involving our nation's greatest president, Abraham Lincoln, he shows just that. In Joshua Wolf Shenk's, *Lincoln's Melancholy* he speaks to the fact that Lincoln "(gave) wide rein to sadness, tenderness, and worry." Most people would say these are weaknesses, but we have to ask the questions: who is he sad for? Who is he tender with? And who does he worry about? It's about someone other than himself, of course. During a trip to Springfield, IL in 1839, Lincoln was in a sizeable group. During the whole ride, he was beside John J. Hardin because they were riding two by two. At one point during the trip, the group took a brief respite in an area surrounded by plum and crabapple trees so that their horses could get something to drink. Before too long, Hardin came back, but the others could not find Lincoln. Hardin said, "oh, when I saw him last, he had caught two little birds in his hand, which the wind had blown from their nest, and he was hunting for the nest." When Lincoln finally came alongside the group again, a number of the men chuckled. To Lincoln, it wasn't a laughing matter. He simply said, "I could not have slept tonight if I had not given those two little birds to their mother."

I had a similar time recently where I was going to struggle throughout my day if I didn't do something for a girl who had some mascara down her face because she had cried after getting into a car accident on the corner of Peachtree Battle & Northside Drive in Buckhead. Something just told me that if I went to the gas station on Defoors Ferry and bought her a 20 oz. Coca-Cola and candy bar, that it would ease her pain of getting into a car accident. When I strode up to her, she probably wondered who I was. I gave her the Hershey's King Size bar and a copy of my first book. She almost started to cry when she said thank you, but she held it in. Hours later, I realized what I accomplished is that instead of focusing on the car accident, she might have been wondering the whole day who on earth I was.

In a Jack Daniels & Coke[12], for every 1 and a half ounces of

---

[12] I encourage you to drink responsibly. Not only will you make better decisions, (anyone who knows me well knows that I have made my fair share of bad decisions when I have had too much to drink) you'll be more productive. Since I published my first book, *Forget Self-Help*, in the fall of 2017, I've

Jack Daniels there is, there is about four and a half ounces of Coca-Cola. You need the sweet taste of Coca-Cola to balance out the strong taste of the Jack. Once you have the combination of the sweet Coke, you cannot only counteract the strong taste of the Jack, you can make it useful; you can turn it into a great drink. As bad as that day was for her, I hope her focus was on the shock of carbonation, caramel color, and sugar, instead of on having to wait on the insurance company to call back.

Although I do not have children of my own at age 30, it's interesting to think about the immense responsibility it will bring to me one day if I am lucky enough to have kids. I was talking recently to a friend from Atlanta who was having fertility problems with his wife. In this particular conversation, I was trying to convince him of a few things. First, I was trying to convince him that parenting is such an immense responsibility because you are literally bringing positivity or negativity into the world. Think about the last ten people you interacted with, people you interacted with that you know well. Do you think of those people in a positive, negative, or neutral light? Chances are you feel very little neutrality towards these people; they either bring a smile or frown to your face. The second thing I tried to convince him of is that the fact that he would or wouldn't be the biological father of the baby had no bearing whatsoever on whether his child would resemble his character and love for people. I've seen in my relationship with Bill McDermott that genes aren't the end all & be all for a son to follow in the footsteps of his father.

---

only gotten drunk once. There's correlation between that fact and the fact that I have written six and a half books since then.

4

Don't Exit Suffering

Like I said earlier, I arrived at Samford University in January of 2009. I had originally attended the University of Alabama, but only for ten days, as I got very sick and had to eventually go back to Atlanta and be immediately admitted to Emory Hospital, where I stayed for ten days. I didn't know what to think of Samford initially when I visited it. It was a beautiful campus, and it seemed to have some pretty girls, so I figured I'd give it a chance. I could have transferred to Gainesville State and eventually matriculated into UGA, but my family, doctors, and I thought a small school would be best.

All my friends from high school seemed to be having the time of their life during their freshman year while I felt like the odd man out. Although the fraternity brothers of Sigma Chi were welcoming, I still missed out on things like inside jokes and the bond that is formed during pledgeship. What made matters worse is that I totaled my car on the way down to Spring Break in Niceville, FL.

Whenever you are suffering, one can certainly be helped by the words of David Brooks in *The Road to Character*. Brooks writes,

For most of us, there is nothing intrinsically noble about suffering. Just as failure is sometimes just failure (and not your path to becoming the next Steve Jobs), suffering is sometimes just as destructive, to be exited or medicated as quickly as possible. When it is not connected to some larger purpose beyond itself, suffering shrinks or annihilates people. When it is not understood as a piece of a larger process, it leads to doubt, nihilism, and despair.

Suffering isn't easy and *choosing* to suffer is even harder. But in life, we must choose to suffer if we ever want anything accomplished. I was too young at the time to remember, but my father taught night law-school in his thirties so we could attend Westminster. There is nothing more noble than to put yourself through pain to ease the pain of someone else.

God calls us to suffer from time to time. That's why *The Purpose-Driven Life*[13] by Rick Warren is such a meaningful book. Much like my first book, *Forget Self-Help: Re-Examining the Golden Rule*, it is the opposite of a self-help book. Proof of this claim is that in the very first chapter, Warren simply tells the reader that life is not about (them.) It's about serving God and others, and, in order to do this, God calls us to suffer from time to time.

One of the times when Jesus gets most disappointed in the New Testament is when the disciples constantly fall asleep despite the fact that he wanted them to keep watch with him:

---

[13] A great book to read if you're struggling with depression.

Then Jesus went with his disciples to a place called Gethsemane, and he said to them, "Sit here while I go over there and pray." He took Peter and the two sons of Zebedee along with him, and he began to be sorrowful and troubled. Then he said to them, "My soul is overwhelmed with sorrow to the point of death. Stay here and keep watch with me." Going a little farther, he fell with his face to the ground and prayed, "My Father, if it is possible, may this cup be taken from me. Yet not as I will, but as you will." Then he returned to his disciples and found them sleeping. "Couldn't you men keep watch with me for one hour?" he asked Peter. "Watch and pray so that you will not fall into temptation. The spirit is willing, but the flesh is weak."

He went away a second time and prayed, "My Father, if it is not possible for this cup to be taken away unless I drink it, may your will be done." When he came back, he again found them sleeping, because their eyes were heavy. So he left them and went away once more and prayed the third time, saying the same thing. Then he returned to the disciples and said to them, "Are you still sleeping and resting? Look, the hour has come, and the Son of Man is delivered into the hands of sinners. Rise! Let us go! Here comes my betrayer!"

Here, Jesus teaches us by far one of the most important lessons in the entire book. It is alright for us to pray to God to alleviate our suffering, but only if it furthers his kingdom or will. If you can do that, you know you are on the path to a close relationship with The Lord.

What's incredible is that even with God on earth encouraging them, the disciples could not stay awake. So often, I, too, struggle to stay awake when God calls me not to sleep. I forget that I'm only fully awake when I am fulfilling His purpose & mission. If you're not suffering in some way or another on a daily basis, then you don't have a close relationship with God.

Don't Idolize Security

For all of the men and women I look up to, security didn't seem to be a part of their vocabulary and, from the person I respect the most, Bill McDermott, whom I will talk about later on in the book, it seems to be a curse word—a word never to be used. Security is the most overrated word in the English language. The reason for this is you cannot suffer when you are secure, and later on in *The Road to Character*, David Brooks says, "recovering from suffering is not like recovering from a disease. Many people don't come out healed; they come out different." To come out different, we must go through pain, and we are not alone in our pain because the Author and Perfector of our Faith went through the exact same pain that we go through on a daily basis, and remember: he chose to do it. If what you're about to attempt doesn't scare you, what you're attempting to do is not of insignificance. Signs on the highway show significant landmarks such as places to eat, stay, and be entertained. Let what you're striving after show the signs of significance as well.

You're No Ham and Egger

We all get afraid from time to time. Fear is natural, but how you respond to fear is what separates the winners from the losers. When you go through something that is about to be true struggle, do not fear, for even Rocky Balboa was afraid to have a shot at the title. Here is the conversation that Rocky has with George Jergens, the promoter of the fight, below.

Jergens: Balboa, George Jergens. Take a chair please. Mr. Balboa.

Rocky: Call me Rocky sir.

Jergens: Tell me Rocky, you've got any representation of a manager?

Rocky: No just me.

Jergens: Rocky I've got a proposition I'd like to make to you.

Rocky: Sparring?

Jergens: I beg your pardon?

Rocky: Well, I'm interested. I know you're looking for sparring partners and I just want to say I'm very available you know.

Jergens: I'm sure you are.

Rocky: Absolutely. Sparring with the champ would be an honor and you know what, Mr. Jergens?

Jergens: What?

Rocky: I wouldn't take no cheap shots either. I'd be a really good sparring partner.

Jergens: You don't understand me, Rocky. My proposition is this. Would you be interested in fighting Apollo Creed for the World Heavyweight Championship?

Rocky: No.

Jergens: Listen Rocky, Apollo's seen you fight. He likes you and he wants to fight you.

Rocky: It's just that you see I fight in clubs you know. I'm really a ham-and-egger and this guy's the best. It wouldn't be such a good fight. Thank you very much though, I appreciate it.

Jergens: Rocky, do you believe that America is the land of opportunity?

Rocky: Yes.

Jergens: Apollo Creed does. He's going to prove it to the whole world by giving an unknown a shot at the title and that unknown is you. He picked you, Rocky. Rocky it's the chance of a lifetime. You can't pass it by. What do you say?

Initially, Rocky thinks he is called in just to be a sparring partner—in other words—on the practice squad. He never thought that he, an uncelebrated unknown, would have a chance at the title. When Rocky is asked by Jergens if he wants a shot, all he says is "no." Jergens tries to convince him again and Rocky isn't having it, telling him, "It's just that you see I fight in clubs you know. I'm really a ham-and-egger and this guy's the best. It wouldn't be such a good fight. Thank you very much though, I appreciate it."

Rocky doesn't want to fight, in part, because he's not only afraid of the struggle, he's afraid he will be embarrassed, and, he knows that if he is embarrassed, he will ultimately suffer. A lot of people told me it took courage to write my first book. I wouldn't necessarily agree with that. I would say that what it took the most is opening myself up to potential suffering, whether that meant that arduous effort it took to write the first book or if the book wasn't received well.

Because I didn't have a PhD or wasn't a pastor, I knew that everyone wasn't expecting much. Rocky was in the same position when he decided to fight Apollo Creed. When Apollo and Rocky have their press conference, Apollo brings up an important event in American history that I brought up earlier: Valley Forge, which was full of suffering. And, even before the press conference, one of the last questions that Jergens asked Rocky is "do you believe that America is the land of opportunity?"

For me, above all, what this movie teaches us is that to have an opportunity to do something memorable, special, noteworthy, or great, one must suffer. I think Roberto Gozuieta, who was CEO of Coca-Cola from 1980-1997, put it best when he said,

> Opportunity always comes accompanies by obligations. In my life, I have found that every opportunity I have ever encountered has implied three fundamental obligations. The first obligation implied in opportunity is that you must seize it... You must reach out to the opportunity... take it in your hands... and mold it into a work that brings value to your society. The second obligation that naturally follows opportunity is that you must live it... you must carry it on your back all day long... you must sense the opportunity in your nostrils with every breath, and you must see it in your dreams when you are asleep... Finally, the third obligation that inherently comes with opportunity is that you must defend it. Squandering what the rest of the world covets is not only foolish... it is immoral. Without action, opportunity

and freedom soon shrivel and fade to a slow death. Opportunity... ours to seize... ours to live... and ours to defend. Or otherwise – ultimately – ours to lose.

The first obligation certainly makes us think. If you are suffering, who are you suffering for? Is it to make more money, move to a nicer address, or purchase any other worldly possessions? If this is the case, your suffering is, more than likely, futile. A man I have come to respect a great deal has challenged me how to truly leave a lasting & valuable mark on society. I met him many years ago on the golf course when I was in high school and looked up to him thereafter from afar. He attended Westminster as well, graduating several years ahead of me. He went to work for a large financial institution in New York City, retiring at age forty, though he could have retired several years earlier.

Noticing that there was a deep problem with homelessness in Atlanta and noticing that government run programs and help from the wealthy wouldn't be enough to help the problem, he created an organization called Georgia Works whose mission was to get the homeless away from addiction and get them to live productive, self-sustainable lives. From time to time over the past several years, I would see posts on social media from the progress they were making. One in particular that struck me was a post with several prominent politicians including Trey Gowdy and Cory Booker.

I had meant to attend a graduation of a class in the past but had never gotten around to it. This year was different; I put it on my calendar. What made the largest impact on me throughout the night was the radiance of hope beaming from each one the graduates. All worries of their past lives were in the rearview mirror; they had gotten the chance to start life anew. I didn't think it at the time, but what Bill McGahan had started several years ago, *that* was what Roberto Goizueta must have meant when he urged us to bring value to society.

*

There is no doubt that in his dream to become the best fighter he can be, Rocky lives it: he carries it on his back all day long, he senses the opportunity in his nostrils with every breath, and he sees it in his dreams when he is asleep. Even when he is not fighting, he is fighting. That's what you must do to get through suffering; that's what you must do to have an impact.

When Rocky is training for the fight, he takes on different things, and he gives up certain things. By doing this, he allows himself to suffer, and, because of this, he gives himself the opportunity to grow stronger; after all, only through suffering can we grow stronger.

He wakes up at 4 AM every single day to train. Breakfast is raw eggs in a cup. From there, he is ready to move, ready to run. When he gets to the top of the stairs, you can tell he is visibly hurt and in intense pain. While some may say he is weak because he got to this point, I say he is strong, because when you have the gall to make yourself weak, you become strong.

Later, Pauli, Rocky's friend, invites him to come to the meat freezer where he works. They talk for a few moments and then Pauli starts to beat one of the chickens because Rocky irritates him somehow. He sees the agony in Pauli's face. While some would stay as far away from the agony and suffering as possible, Rocky seems drawn to it because he knows it will make him stronger. In *The Road to Character*, David Brooks writes that, "suffering opens up ancient places of pain that had been hidden. It exposes frightening experiences that had been repressed, shameful wrongs that had been committed. It spurs some people to painfully and carefully examine the basement of their own soul." If there was ever a time to do this, it was in preparing for the fight of his life.

*

To squander is ultimately to waste. What's interesting is that waste, a synonym of squander, is both a verb and noun; in other words, when you waste, you produce waste. When you squander something, you're not producing something valueless; in some ways, you're producing something of intrinsic negative value because whatever you produce has to be stored and kept at a cost. Earlier, in *Rocky*, Jergens tells Rocky, "it's the chance of a lifetime. You can't pass it by. What do you say?" More than anything, what Rocky knew he needed was persistence, and, as Ray Kroc says in the movie *The Founder*:

Persistence. Nothing in the world can take the place of persistence. Talent won't. Nothing is more common than unsuccessful men with talent. Genius won't. Unrewarded genius is practically a cliché. Education won't. The world is full of educated fools. Persistence and determination alone are all powerful. Show that you don't have to be defeated by anything. That you can have peace of mind, improved health and a never ceasing flow of energy. If you attempt each and every day to achieve these things, the results will make themselves obvious to you. While it may sound like a magical notion, it is in you to create your own future. The greatest discovery of my generation is that human beings can alter their lives by altering their attitudes of mind. Or as

Ralph Waldo Emerson declared, "A man is what he thinks about all day long."

What you think about determines your steps. What your steps determine is where you'll end up. Are you going to end up squandering what you think about, which is ultimately going to determine where you end up? Instead of thinking about all the hours you waste pursuing your dream, why not try so you won't be a waste?

What do Donald Trump, Mitt Romney, and George W. Bush have in common with me? Well, there are a few things. First, we all Republicans, although I consider myself to be a little bit more moderate than them. Second, we all came from very privileged backgrounds, attending elite private schools and didn't have to worry about student loans when it came to paying for college. There's one thing that differentiates myself from them, though: I admit this fact freely. I got a clear head-start in life. If I ever hit a homerun in life, I'll not only admit to starting on third base; I'll tell people that I was born sliding into home.

While you probably don't have the same financial advantages I had, there's a chance you have something that is better than another person. How are you using those advantages? Remember that, as I say in *Forget Self-Help*, "When people speak of having an advantage over someone, they often feel as if they have to tread on sharp glass. There is no need to do this because none of us created our own advantages. They were given to us by God. However, we do need to tread lightly on how we use our advantages to help others." You might have the ability to listen, to make people feel welcomed, you might be attractive, you might be able to cook; whatever it is, make sure you are using it to further society—and yourself in some cases—instead of using the advantage in a destructive manner.

Be of Value

I received my bid to Sigma Chi the following fall and was told that when my picture came up on the screen for the brothers to vote, melee ensued, with one brother stripping down to his underwear to show his support of me. Despite the fact that I already knew all of the brothers and had been on multiple trips with some, I took pledgeship seriously, placing third when we were initiated out of some fifteen to twenty pledges.

When I became a brother, people appreciated my loyalty, integrity, friendliness, and respect for custodians whether they consisted of the workers in the cafeteria or janitors cleaning up the house. Luckily, they put up with my pretentiousness as I was the only brother from Buckhead and was probably overly proud of my Alma Mater, Westminster. Anybody who was alive in the fraternity also knew I had a deep appreciation for Robert E. Lee[14], *To Kill a Mockingbird*, and Abita Purple Haze beer.

Above all, however, people in the fraternity grew to respect my wisdom. My pledge class nickname soon became "Father Fellows" among our class and sweethearts, Angela Stout and Weathers Veazey. My junior year, there became a heated debate on whether or not we were going to kick out a pledge. People expressed different sentiments about what to do, but nobody took the debate as seriously as I did; no one else took the time to write up what they were going to say. During my talk, I talked about the importance

---

[14] Of course not his views on race or the fact that he fought for the South

of discipline, harkening back to my days working at the prestigious Peachtree Golf Club in Atlanta when my boss was hard on me and why I was thankful for that. I believe I also quoted my favorite verse[15] of the Bible of all time, Hebrews 12:11, which reads, "No discipline is pleasant at the time, but it later produces a harvestful of righteousness and peace for those who are trained by it."

The talk must have hit one of the brothers hard because he came up to me and apologized. Remember that night I told you about when everyone cheered when my name came up on the board? Apparently, there was one who argued against my admission. Coincidentally, his good friend back home in Alabama happened to be my roommate when I fell ill in Alabama. Because I was acting out of the norm while I was there, he told his friend who was a member of Sigma Chi not to take a chance on me. To be honest, this member of Sigma Chi had always treated me well, but it wasn't until I truly proved to be a value to the fraternity that he apologized.

Nassir Ghaemi, who I mentioned in the first chapter, writes in a *First Rate-Madness* that he suspects the deep cultural stigma accompanying mental illness may be among our species' deepest biases, more so than even sexism and racism. Luckily, my fraternity brother saw me as Thomas Fellows, the fraternity brother, and not Thomas Fellows, the one, who by the end of my time with them, was on five medications—all for mental health.

---

[15] In 2008, then pastor of Peachtree Presbyterian Vic Pentz had us put our favorite Bible verses on a bumper sticker and stick it on an Old VW Van. Of course, my sticker read Hebrews 12:11.

5

Wider and Fairer to Me

Have you ever appreciated a person who told you that you expect too much of them? I've mentioned this in other books, but when I first came out with *Forget Self-Help*, hardly any of my male mentors took the time to read and appreciate my book. There was one person who was different, however, it was Bill McDermott. McDermott is now present-day CEO of ServiceNow, an American cloud computing company with their headquarters in Santa Clara, CA. He was co-CEO and CEO of SAP, where he increased its market value from $39 billion to $156 billion in just 16 years. Prior to that, he served in various senior leadership roles at Xerox.

Getting back to the original question: have you ever dealt with a person or people like that? How does that make you feel? In some cases, this can be valid, such as the other day when someone who I had never met before connected with me through a mutual friend that I didn't know all that well and asked for me to read his book and post a review online[16]. That would be people-pleasing

---

[16] Ironically, if I had done the review, it might have helped me close some business because I saw on LinkedIn because he was connected with some prospects. Bill McDermott actually made this point in a talk he did at the

to do unless I had been really interested in the subject, and Galatians 1:10 says, "For am I now seeking the approval of man, or of God? Or am I trying to please man? If I were still trying to please man, I would not be a servant of Christ."

Some of the people were actively involved in the book, whether they were in it or acknowledged, and, still, I did not hear a word from them. These were people who demand very little of themselves rather than demand too much of themselves. Bill McDermott is someone who demands too much of himself, which is why I look up to him both as a role-model and surrogate father. Another Bill, this one by the name of Bill Pressly, founder of The Westminster Schools in Atlanta, GA, said something interesting about "demanding too much" in *The Formative Years*, a book he wrote about the school's early years. Here it is below:

> Most criticism that Westminster is a "pressure cooker" probably comes from persons associated with other schools. Westminster's record has been so superior they've felt we required too much of students. Most of Westminster's parents, however, haven't taken these statements seriously.
>
> Of course, some Westminster teachers have, indeed, required too much. An ambitious teacher wants to challenge students as much as possible. Occasionally, he or she steps out of bounds and demands too much, not an uncommon

---

Fuqua School of Business at Duke University. He has done two talks there, one in 2013 and one in 2018. I honestly forget which one he said this in.

mistake by any by any good teacher.

A relative and I were going back and forth a year or two ago about whether Westminster was a good fit for me; she knew the fact that I struggled mightily there. Because I struggled mightily, she made the assumption that it was not the right place for me. That was the wrong assumption to make. There, I learned to demand too much of myself, which is a quality I soon learned I shared with my mentor Bill.

Because I struggled, I got used to failing at a young age, and, as Nassir Ghaemi writes in a *First-Rate Madness*, "of course, everyone suffers. But life's pain can come harshly or gently, earlier or later. For the lucky, suffering is less frequent, less severe, and delayed until it can't be avoided. The unlucky, who, early in their lives, endure hardships and tragedies—or the challenge of mental illness—seem to become, not infrequently, our greatest leaders."

When I pledged Sigma Chi at Samford, for me, compared to most of the rest of the pledge class, pledgeship seemed like a breeze. Memorizing certain passages from the pledge handbook was easy compared to having powerful foreign substances in your body affecting every step.

While Bill McDermott doesn't struggle with mental illness, to get where he is today—making 8-figures a year—was no easy task. If any quote defines McDermott, it is his epigraph in his autobiography, *Winners Dream: A Journey from the Corner Store to the Corner Office*, which is a quote that Robert F. Kennedy said at the University of Kansas in 1968 when he quoted George Bernard Shaw

76

saying, "Some people see things as they are and say, why? I dream things that never were and say, why not?"

Part 1 of McDermott's biography is entitled "Hungry." McDermott was born in Flushing, New York in the borough of Queens. During the first ten years of his life, he lived in a succession of working-class neighborhoods such as College Point, Hicksville, Babylon, and Brentwood—all blue-collar towns where his parents moved them from one rental apartment to another. Finally, they saved up enough money to buy a home, whereupon dead squirrels and rats were found in the walls once they started to fix it up. Psychiatrist Victor Frankl once noted that

> the way in which a man accepts his fate and all the suffering it entails, the way in which he takes up his cross, gives him ample opportunity—even under the most difficult circumstances—to add a deeper meaning to his life. It may remain brave, dignified and unselfish. Or in the bitter fight for self-preservation he may forget his human dignity and become no more than an animal. Here lies the chance for a man either to make use of or to forgo the opportunities of attaining the moral values that a difficult situation may afford him. And this decides whether he is worthy of his sufferings or not.

When the McDermott's bought their first home, massive renovations had to be made, with friends and family lending a hand when needed. McDermott writes, "for my parents, homeownership was a step up and a great source of pride. For me, it was home, and the happiest place in the world, despite its imperfections."

Having a sense of pride—especially after it entails a great deal of suffering to accomplish what one has accomplished—makes the world not only turn on its axis, but also keeps us from getting swept away into the atmosphere. According to Dr. Sten Odenweld of NASA, "if the Earth stopped spinning suddenly, the atmosphere would still be in motion with the Earth's original 1100 mile per hour rotation speed at the equator. All of the land masses would be scoured clean of anything not attached to bedrock. This means rocks, topsoil, trees, buildings, your pet dog, and so on, would be swept away into the atmosphere." If we, as a people, are not attached to suffering in one form or another, all will be swept away. We must choose to suffer everyday; after all, Romans 5:3-5 says, "we (should) also glory in our sufferings, because we know that suffering produces perseverance; perseverance, character; and character, hope. And hope does not put us to shame, because God's love has been poured out into our hearts through the Holy Spirit, who has been given to us." As our suffering produces character, so, too, does it produce hope because what seems without reach with just man is always within grasp with God.

*

When Bill McDermott entered management at the young age of 24 at Xerox, he stepped into the shoes of his team and tried to incentivize and encourage them as he did for himself. Instead of just encouraging them to hit their number, in order to liberate them, he tried to have his reps think of tangible items such as buying a car or a house. Because he expected too much of himself to begin with, he was able to pass on that same level of intensity to his reps. In short, he pushed them, and as one piece in the *Sangamo Journal*, during the era of Abraham Lincoln on "how to succeed" says,

Push along. Push hard. Push earnestly ... You can't do without it. The world is so made — society is so constructed that it's a law of necessity that you must push. That is if you want to be something and somebody.

Who succeeds? Who makes money, honor, and reputation? He who heartily, sincerely, manfully *pushed* and *he only*. Be what you may at the top or bottom of the scale, you have got to *push* in it to command success. It's so with every man. Do you point to what is called the man of *genius?* And you think he doesn't *push?* Why, he's your companion pusher — he pushes all the time. It's the very philosophy of his height and power ...

If things look dark, push harder. — Sunshine and blue sky are just beyond. If you are entangled, push — if your heart grows feeble, push, push. You'll come out glorious, never fear. You are on the right track, and working with right materials. So push along, keep pushing.

While Tom Lincoln, Abraham's father, was content with being average, his son was not. In *Lincoln's Melancholy*, Joshua Wolf Shenk writes, "(Lincoln) saw wages as a kind of liberation. When he was a teenager, Lincoln kept a skiff on the Ohio River, a thoroughfare of the American market. One day two men hired him to row them out to a larger boat. Lincoln expected "a few bits" in payment, but as the men climbed out, they threw back two silver half-dollars. "I could scarcely believe my eyes," Lincoln recalled when he was president. "Gentlemen, you may think it was a little thing ... but it was the most important incident in my life. I could scarcely credit that I, a poor boy, had earned a dollar in less than a day ... The world seemed wider and fairer to me."

Before explaining how similar this statement is to McDermott's own recounting of his young life, I first have to explain how the world seemed wider and fairer to me after I sold bottled water at Chastain Park Ampitheatre on the very North side of Atlanta. When I was in high-school, I sold bottled water there for concerts, which happened three or four times a week before the Verizon Wireless Ampitheatre in Alpharetta took many shows away from it. I sold the water with Will Coleman[17], who was a neighbor and fellow Westminster student.

We prided ourselves in buying Dasani, the Coke brand water, as opposed to Kroger water. We also dressed up differently to appeal to our customers depending on who was playing. Like Lincoln, I remember those nights with great fondness. We certainly didn't *have* to sell bottled water considering we lived in Buckhead and both went to the same prestigious private school. But we chose to work hard, and there was a certain amount of pleasure in divvying up the night's earnings, which consisted of wet, wadded up one, five, ten, and twenty-dollar bills.

*

Later, in *Winners Dream*, Bill McDemrott writes,

---

[17] When I was 6 or 7 years old, and Will saw me playing baseball instead of selling lemonade, he asked me why I wasn't at my job (which he of course thought was selling lemonade.)

Even my brother, Kevin, who was tougher around the edges than I was, agreed that my family generated enough love to fill a mansion. So instead of feeling angry that my parents were putting me in Skips sneakers from the dollar store instead of cooler Pumas, I put myself in their shoes. I believed that they deserved better. Not better in terms of material possessions—although they wanted to get me Pumas even more than I wanted those shoes for myself—but better stability. After seeing how much my parents gave and how little they got, I could not let that go on for another generation.

Maybe I could empathize with my parents because I was their oldest child, or because of how I was hardwired, or maybe because my mother repeatedly told me, often in the same breath, that "anything worthwhile in life does not come easy" and that "you have the potential to do anything you set your mind to." Whatever the reasons, I wanted to come through for my family, to protect them when they got clobbered with crisis. What's more, I'd been given, and was maybe even born with, enough confidence to believe I could do it. And even though I wasn't starving and my parents weren't asking for money, I saw money as a way to give myself financial independence and to give my parents the security that they gave me with their love. I wanted to be their Saint Jude.

One of the most incorrectly quoted Bible verses of all time is 1st Timothy 6:10, which reads, "For the love of money is the root of all evil: which while some coveted after, they have erred from the faith, and pierced themselves through with many sorrows." Many people incorrectly leave out "for the love of" and, instead, simply say "money is the root of all evil." Money, rightfully earned with hard work, is the backbone of the American democracy. In the next chapter, in which I will describe my long stint of unemployment, I will speak to what it did to my morale, my confidence, not earning money. When I went on a micro-lending mission trip to South Africa several years ago, I learned that our chief purpose was to get the people working again and off federal aid.

Refusing to Just Dig a Hole

One of the most powerful parables that Jesus told was the Parable of the Talents in Matthew 25:14-30. It reads,

> "Again, it will be like a man going on a journey, who called his servants and entrusted his wealth to them. To one he gave five bags of gold, to another two bags, and to another one bag, each according to his ability. Then he went on his journey. The man who had received five bags of gold went at once and put his money to work and gained five bags more. So also, the one with two bags of gold gained two more. But the man who had received one bag went off, dug a hole in the ground and hid his master's money.
>
> After a long time the master of those servants returned and settled accounts with them. The man who had received five bags of gold brought the other five. 'Master,'

he said, 'you entrusted me with five bags of gold. See, I have gained five more.'

His master replied, 'Well done, good and faithful servant! You have been faithful with a few things; I will put you in charge of many things. Come and share your master's happiness!'

The man with two bags of gold also came. 'Master,' he said, 'you entrusted me with two bags of gold; see, I have gained two more.'

"His master replied, 'Well done, good and faithful servant! You have been faithful with a few things; I will put you in charge of many things. Come and share your master's happiness!'

Then the man who had received one bag of gold came. 'Master,' he said, 'I knew that you are a hard man, harvesting where you have not sown and gathering where you have not scattered seed. So I was afraid and went out and hid your gold in the ground. See, here is what belongs to you.'

His master replied, 'You wicked, lazy servant! So you knew that I harvest where I have not sown and gather where I have not scattered seed? Well then, you should have put my money on deposit with the bankers, so that when I returned I would have received it back with interest.
"So take the bag of gold from him and give it to the

one who has ten bags. For whoever has will be given more, and they will have an abundance. Whoever does not have, even what they have will be taken from them. And throw that worthless servant outside, into the darkness, where there will be weeping and gnashing of teeth.'

Bill McDermott was not like the man who just hid his talent in the ground. With whatever he had, he made sure to grow it, not into another talent, but many more than that. McDermott, in his biography, would later say, "having a steady job and money saved gave me a sense of control in my unpredictable world. After doing a few other jobs, such as baby-sitting and other odd jobs, at age fifteen, a Finast supermarket opened up in town." Much like I will explain in the next chapter, when I was getting my first job back after a lengthy stint of unemployment, McDermott showed the boss that he wanted the job more than any of his competition, who had more experience and age on him. He told the store manager, Mr. Kelly, "Hi Mr. Kelly, I'm Bill McDermott. I just want you to know that I waited in line for the last hour to submit my application because I really want to work here. Sir, I guarantee that if you give me this job, I'll work very hard for you. I just need a chance."

Even though the applicant line was still down the block, when McDermott got home, which was less than a mile away, his mother called him to tell him the staff from Finast was on the phone. Mr. Kelly told him, "Bill, we think you have a lot of energy. You can start tomorrow." During my time of knowing Bill, which has been nearly five years now, he lives out these words from Victor Frankl better than anyone I know: "it didn't really matter what we expected from life, but rather what life expected from us." Proof is in the below paragraph:

I graduated from the parking lot to stocking shelves. The day I accidentally cut my hand with a box cutter as I sliced open a carton full of canned goods, a coworker drove me to the hospital and waited while they stitched me up. I was back at Finast within a few hours. The way I saw it, I owed Finast at least ninety minutes. Plus, I wanted to prove that my injury wouldn't stop me from completing my stocking duties, and get me demoted to collected carts.

I took every job seriously, and whether I was stacking cans in a supermarket smock, digging dirt in muddy shorts, or delivering papers in my school clothes, I started to develop basic work habits. By maximizing my time, being polite and conscientious, staying true to my word, showing up on time, and holding myself accountable, I was acting like a professional before I had to look like one. I was "wearing the jacket" long before I could afford or need a real jacket of my own. I understood that whether someone's pay was hourly or salaried, his collar blue or white, professional work habits alone wouldn't get people promoted, but a lack of professionalism wouldn't get people anywhere. So even when my jobs were small, I acted big.

My favorite part of reading biographies or Wikipedia pages has always been the formative years of that person's life. The reason for that is it always sets the foundation for that person's life—how they are going to live. When I sent that cold email telling McDermott to check his LinkedIn messages, I gave him a brief update on what I had been doing in my software sales career, but more importantly, I told him how I started my career in sales as a young kid. I bet if you were to ask him what made him get me in touch with a recruiter, it was that while my jobs as a young kid were small, I acted big.

6

Stranded (But Not on a Deserted Island)

I would never wish anyone to be stranded on a deserted island, nor would I wish anyone to be unemployed. Mokokoma Mokhonoana once said, "when you are unemployed, weekends are seven days long." On the last day of March 2018, I got the news that I either would have to move up to Chicago to continue working for my company or look for work elsewhere. Since I had already exhausted my list of people to call, and the company was tiny, I decided to stay in Atlanta and look for work. The main problem I found myself having was that I was either overqualified or under-qualified for jobs; my skill-set of cold-calling was useful to companies, but many companies were weary to take me on given the vast number of companies had worked for and the short stints I had worked for each one of them.

After many interviews with no luck, I decided to try an alternative to sales. I decided I would work for Walmart in a physical store and eventually work my way into a corporate job in Benton-ville, Arkansas. When I found out that there were four executives there that made 8-figures annually, I was even more intrigued because for quite some time I had wanted to make 8-figures. When I interviewed, even though the job didn't require a college education, knowing my luck, I thought somehow I might not get the job. Luckily, that didn't happen, and I got the job. When I started work, I didn't feel trapped anymore; I felt as if there was light at the end of the tunnel. I had a friend from college whose father had worked high-up at Walmart previously. The plan was going to be for him to get me a job in Bentonville. Unfortunately, that plan never came to fruition.

The thing I am most thankful for at Walmart was that it helped me empathize with my fellow human beings more than I ever had from a socio-economic standpoint. Prior to Walmart, I never fathomed people running out of money for basic necessities; I had never lived paycheck to paycheck as they were doing now. Although I've always considered myself a capitalist, seeing the way some of my customers and fellow employees were forced to live reminded me of a little-known Adam Smith[18] quote where he says in the *Wealth of Nations*, "what improves the circumstances of the greater part can never be regarded as an inconveniency to the whole. No society can surely be flourishing and happy, of which the far greater part of the members are poor and miserable."

We'll get back to how my unemployment ended—it's really quite a story—but, for now, let's examine how miserable Jim Preston, a character in the 2016 movie *Passengers* must have been when he realized he was stranded on a spaceship because he accidentally woke up years before he was supposed to.

---

[18] Adam Smith is widely known father of Capitalism.

When Jim boarded the spaceship Avalon, he thought he was going to get a chance at a new life, a new start. Unfortunately, his hibernation pod that he was supposed to be sleeping in for 120 years malfunctioned. When he wakes up and goes to his orientation class, there is one thing that is terribly wrong: he realizes that he is the only one awake aboard the ship.

One of the first conversations that Jim has is with a bartender, who turns out to be just a robot. Here's part of the conversation below:

> **Jim Preston** : How long until we get to Homestead II?
> **Arthur** : About ninety years or so.
> **Jim Preston** : And when are all the passengers supposed to wake up?
> **Arthur** : Not till the last four months.
> **Jim Preston** : *[cheerily]* How is it that I'm sitting here with you? With ninety years to go?
> **Arthur** : *[after glitching for a moment]* Hm. It's not possible for you to be here.
> **Jim Preston** : Well, I am.

I had a similar thought after my most recent interview with a tech payroll company didn't work out. Originally, I was supposed to have four interviews; I ended up having five, with the last one being dangerously similar to hazing, but at the end, the person on the other line said, "Thomas, remember this day, because five years from now, know that I knew you were going to be an all-star." Still, I did not get the job, more than likely because I was overqualified once again—the word I was beginning to dread most. I decided I would expand my search and try San Francisco. I flew out there and ended up interviewing with a few companies but got neither

89

job. In June and July, I tried Raleigh. I thought I got one job with a large IT company, but was again denied. Nick Tzitzon of SAP offered to help me get a job with Qualtrics, who had just been bought out by SAP, but I decided that I would stay in Atlanta. You might be wondering why I didn't get a job at SAP where Bill McDermott was CEO. There were reasons why I couldn't do this: First, if I worked for SAP, it would eventually have gotten around that I knew him well, making it a nightmare situation for my manager. Secondly, there would have been a legal problem because SAP does not permit nepotism.[19]

Speaking of a problem, in *Passengers*, Jim has one main problem: loneliness. Later, when talking to Arthur, the two of them have a conversation. Here it is below:

> **Jim Preston**: So lay some bartender wisdom on me. I'm lost in space here.
> **Arthur**: You're not where you want to be. You feel like you're supposed to be somewhere else. Well, say you could snap your fingers and be wherever you wanted to be... I bet you'd still feel this way: Not in the right place. The point is you can't get so hung up on where you'd rather be that you forget to make the most of where you are.
> **Jim Preston**: What are you telling me?
> **Arthur**: Take a break from worrying about what you can't control. Live a little.

---

[19] Patronage bestowed or favoritism shown on the basis of family relationship, as in business and politics.

Jim does decide to "live a little", but in the scenes that ensue, all involve him *taking* instead of *giving*, and, because of that, they leave him unfulfilled. There are scenes of him playing basketball, dancing, ordering way more food than he should order, and the last scene involves him having far too many margaritas. Some of my favorite quotes from my first book, *Forget Self-Help*, are below:

> *When we do for others, we provide more happiness for ourselves more effectively than when we try to focus only on ourselves. The reason for this is simple: putting ourselves in another's shoes makes us forget all about our own problems.*

> *I've learned throughout life that you will never regret giving a part of yourself for someone else whether that be time or money.*

Unfortunately for Jim, what both of these quotes involve is another person, and, because he is stranded, he doesn't have that luxury.

*

In one of the most famous short stories of all time, "To Build a Fire," by Jack London, there is a man who travels on the Yukon trail alone with a dog who helps him to navigate. Just like Jim, he faced strife:

> There was no sun or promise of sun, although there was not a cloud in the sky. It was a clear day. However, there seemed to be an indescribable darkness over the face of things. That was because the sun was absent from the sky. This fact did not worry the man. He was not alarmed by the

lack of sun. It had been days since he had seen the sun.

    The man is supposed to be at camp to see the "boys" at 6 o' clock, but he soon realizes—through a series of bad blunders—that he will get there in time. Much to the dog's great delight, the man decides to build a fire, and it becomes a roaring one, warming both the dog and man.

    Unfortunately, later, the man falls into a creek, which he knew could be a death sentence with it being 75 degrees below freezing. Later, the short story reads,

> He remembered the advice of the old man on Sulphur Creek, and smiled. The man had been very serious when he said that no man should travel alone in that country after 50 below zero. Well, here he was; he had had the accident; he was alone; and he had saved himself. Those old men were rather womanish, he thought. All a man must do was to keep his head, and he was all right. Any man who was a man could travel alone.

    The man was not the only one to realize he could not travel alone; in *Passengers*, Jim realized this as well. After a meal, Jim decides to go to the top level of the spaceship and realizes that he, too, can go into space. He jumps into the spacesuit and goes into space, tethered to the ship to make sure he doesn't get away. To get into space is supposed to be a joy, it is supposed to be a thrill, but alone, it's meaningless. After he comes back, he ultimately realizes that his life, too, is void of meaning, and considers jumping off the ship to end his life. At the last second, he decides not to jump. In prisons, prisoners who are given the worst punishment are forced to go into solitary confinement. If this is indeed the case, Jim is a prisoner with the worst punishment for another 89 years.

Just as when he seems to give up on life altogether, he has a thought, an idea, which seems like the only way he could be possibly survive. When I'm suffering, I've noticed to better my mood, I've got to appreciate the little things, another spark that could give me the feeling that the present suffering I am going through could cease. A song that has helped me do that through the years is "Warehouse" by the Dave Matthews Band. In the most poignant part of the song, Dave sings, "Keep all the illumination going, so we can see the dark feline changing shades, and we can stroll under ladders, and we can wade as the current spins you around in the right direction."

To be spun in the right direction, sometimes you've got to let the current do its own work instead of swimming against it; after all, in a 2017 *New York Times* article entitled "How to Survive a Rip Current: First, Don't Fight It," Maggie Astor writes, "when being swept out to sea, most people's first instinct will be to fight the current. Don't. Rip currents can move eight feet per second, and you cannot: The fastest human swimmers can typically go only about 5.4 feet per second, and that's at a sprint. If you try to swim against the current, all you will do is exhaust yourself. That would probably be true even for an Olympic swimmer." What does Astor suggest to do instead? "The key fact to remember is that rip currents, powerful as they are, tend to be narrow. If you are caught in one, swim parallel to the shore until you break out of it. Then follow the waves, at an angle, back to land."

It's interesting that Astor says that rip currents are narrow.

Many times, we don't realize that rather than suffering being wide and elongated, it can be escaped if we tell ourselves to work smarter instead of harder. Ted Turner once said, "Confronted with a problem, I've always looked for an unconventional angle and approach. Nothing sneaky, nothing illegal or unethical, just turning the issue on its head and shifting the advantage to our side." In the same way, Romans 12:2 tells us, "Do not conform to the pattern of this world, but be transformed by the renewing of your mind. Then you will be able to test and approve what God's will is—his good, pleasing and perfect will." There is no more thing pleasing to the Lord than to choose to suffer by doing it; after all, Matthew 5:11 says, "Blessed are you when people insult you, persecute you, and falsely say all kinds of evil against you because of me." Only when you begin to choose to suffer from time to time do you know your faith is catching on. If you find yourself seeking pleasure all the time instead of pain, check yourself because not only do sacrifice and suffering start with the same letter, but they also both bring a smile to God.

*

Earlier, we talked about Jim's insistence on having someone alive aboard the ship. After spending much time deciding whether or not to wake the girl of his dreams, Aurora, up, he gives into the temptation, knowing she will be just as stranded as he. Aurora wakes up and becomes acquainted with Jim, knowing that she is to be stranded on the ship for the next 88 years. When she goes to her cabin to go to sleep for the first night, she says something ironic to Jim: "More than a year? I can't imagine. It must have been so hard for you." Jim's only response is, "it was."

A Problem to Solve

Aurora's a writer, specifically, a journalist. She demands Jim answer why he decided to board the ship, Avalon, in the first place. Being a mechanic, Jim tells her, "Back on earth, when something breaks, you don't fix it, you replace it. You know the colonies, they have problems to solve, they're my type of problems. A mechanic is someone; a new world is still being built." What's interesting is that Jim finds meaning and purpose in helping other people out, not just himself. When you're suffering, you naturally think that first and foremost you must dig yourself out of a hole, when in actuality, digging other people out of a hole can prove to be much more effective for alleviating that suffering.

Aurora digs Jim out of that hole with her mere existence. She's beautiful—both in the way of the girl next door and in the way of the homecoming queen. They learn to suffer with one another, and in the words of John Winthrop in *A Model for Christian Charity*, "we must delight in each other, make others' conditions our own, rejoice together, mourn together, labor, and suffer together, always having before our eyes our commission and community in the work, our community as members of the same body." I never played football at Westminster, but I remember distinctly that the football team went down to Cocoa Beach every summer for a week to practice. Florida in July is miserable, with the temperatures hovering in the low to mid-nineties and high humidity. Early on in high school, it was considered "cool" to play football; all the popular kids did it. My friends used to complain about it, but I know deep down they were proud to be part of the team.

In the same light, Aurora writes in her new book, "Jim and I live in 'accidental happiness,' like castaways making their home in strange shores. We all have dreams. We plan our futures like we're the captains of our fate, but we're passengers. We go where fate takes us. This isn't the life we planned, but it's ours. And for the first time in my life, I don't feel alone. We weren't supposed to find each other, but we did. He makes me feel like my life isn't over. It's just beginning." In many ways we can't choose the fate that God has given us. Some of are born tall, some of us are born short, some of us white, some of us black. What we can do, however, is react to what God has given us because he has given us free will. We are not robots programmed by God; we have choices. Whatever problems you are going through, know that in the end, you have a choice as to how you will react to it.

Getting back to "To Build a Fire," after a failed fire that would have saved his life, the man had an idea:

The sight of the dog put a wild idea into his head. He remembered the story of the man, caught in a storm, who killed an animal and sheltered himself inside the dead body and thus was saved. He would kill the dog and bury his hands in the warm body until feeling returned to them. Then he could build another fire.

He spoke to the dog, calling it to him. But in his voice a

strange note of fear that frightened the animal. It had never known the man to speak in such a tone before. Something was wrong and it sensed danger. It knew not what danger, but somewhere in its brain arose a fear of the man. It flattened its ears at the sound of the man's voice; its uneasy movements and the liftings of its feet became more noticeable. But it would not come to the man. He got down on his hands and knees and went toward the dog. But this unusual position again excited fear and the animal moved away.

The man sat in the snow for a moment and struggled for calmness. Then he pulled on his mittens, using his teeth, and then stood on his feet. He glanced down to assure himself that he was really standing, because lack of feeling in his feet gave him no relation to the earth. His position, however, removed the fear from the dog's mind.

When he commanded the dog with his usual voice, the dog obeyed and came to him. As it came within his reach, the man lost control. His arms stretched out to hold the dog and he experienced real surprise when he discovered that his hands could not grasp. There was neither bend nor feeling in the fingers. He had forgotten for the moment that they were frozen and that they were freezing more and more. All this happened quickly and before the animal could escape, he encircled its body with his arms. He sat down in the snow, and in this fashion held the dog, while it barked and struggled.

But it was all he could do: hold its body encircled in his arms and sit there. He realized that he could not kill the dog. There was no way to do it. With his frozen hands he could neither draw nor hold his knife. Nor could he grasp the dog around the throat. He freed it and it dashed wildly away, still barking. It stopped 40 feet away and observed him curiously, with ears sharply bent forward.

While the man didn't want to hurt a human, but rather a dog, the same principle applies. Andy Stanley (and possibly others) once said, "Hurt people hurt people." That's why Jim woke Aurora out of hibernation; that's why Bob Ewell in *To Kill a Mockingbird* is so racist; that's why insecure people abuse others. Our first inclination is to look out for ourselves when we are suffering, and, when we do so, it often causes us to forget to look out for the needs of others. Christ, on the other hand, got hurt on the cross so that he could *help* people. He didn't have to do so, but he wanted to make us whole again.

*

Later, in *Passengers*, Aurora finds out through Arthur, the bartender, that the only reason she is up is because Jim woke her up. She's certainly dismayed and refuses to talk to Jim for quite some time. She finally starts to communicate with him when he realizes that she must team up with him to save the ship that is in the process of breaking down completely. At one point, she asks Jim, "What are we looking for?" Jim responds with, "Something broken. Something big." Sometimes, the reason God wants us to suffer is to get that big part of us that is off the track back on the rails. He does this because this is the only way we will be able to see what we are doing wrong. Are you wise enough to realize this? I hope so.

*

Jim realizes that to save the ship, he has to risk his own life for Aurora. When Jim leaves to go to outer space to fix the ship, the respect that Aurora has for Jim is restored. In many ways, at that moment, Jim finally becomes the man that Aurora has always longed for. It reminds me of this poem by Rudyard Kipling:

> If you can keep your head when all about you
> Are losing theirs and blaming it on you,
> If you can trust yourself when all men doubt you,
> But make allowance for their doubting too;
> If you can wait and not be tired by waiting,
> Or being lied about, don't deal in lies,
> Or being hated, don't give way to hating,
> And yet don't look too good, nor talk too wise:
>
> If you can dream—and not make dreams your master;
> If you can think—and not make thoughts your aim;
> If you can meet with Triumph and Disaster
> And treat those two impostors just the same;
> If you can bear to hear the truth you've spoken
> Twisted by knaves to make a trap for fools,
> Or watch the things you gave your life to, broken,
> And stoop and build 'em up with worn-out tools:
>
> If you can make one heap of all your winnings

And risk it on one turn of pitch-and-toss,
And lose, and start again at your beginnings
And never breathe a word about your loss;
If you can force your heart and nerve and sinew
To serve your turn long after they are gone,
And so hold on when there is nothing in you
Except the Will which says to them: 'Hold on!'

If you can talk with crowds and keep your virtue,
Or walk with Kings—nor lose the common touch,
If neither foes nor loving friends can hurt you,
If all men count with you, but none too much;
If you can fill the unforgiving minute
With sixty seconds' worth of distance run,
Yours is the Earth and everything that's in it,
And—which is more—you'll be a Man, my son!

Contrary to what popular culture tells us, being a man is not about chewing tobacco, drinking beer, or having a gun, it's about doing things that require a condition of bravery, which is what the poem, "If" is all about. The poet, Rudyard Kipling, knew that "if moments" require someone to go beyond the normal act of duty are into a space reserved only for the heroic.

There are two lines in particular that "show a gentleman in plain light," as Robert E. Lee would say. They are: "Or being lied about, don't deal in lies/Or being hated, don't give way to hating." How frustrating is it to be lied about? It's just about the most frustrating thing in the world. Abraham Lincoln once said, "Neither let us be slandered from our duty by false accusations against us, nor frightened from it by menaces of destruction to the government, nor of dungeons to ourselves. Let us have faith that right makes might, and in that faith let us to the end dare to do our duty as we understand it."

Here's the thing about people who are spreading unjust rumors or lies about you: they probably aren't going anywhere to begin with. I've been shocked at the response by some of my friends at the lack of praise for my book success. If I had a friend who had been on five medications starting in his twenties, been suicidal twice, and has had his fair share of family issues, I would be overjoyed for what he had overcome.

*

In what is one of the most misunderstood Bible passages of all time, Ephesians 5:22-33 says,

> Wives, submit yourselves to your own husbands as you do to the Lord. For the husband is the head of the wife as Christ is the head of the church, his body, of which he is the Savior. Now as the church submits to Christ, so also wives should submit to their husbands in everything.
>
> Husbands, love your wives, just as Christ loved the church and gave himself up for her to make her holy, cleansing her by the washing with water through the word, and to present her to himself as a radiant church, without stain or wrinkle or any other blemish, but holy and blameless. In this same way, husbands ought to love their

wives as their own bodies. He who loves his wife loves himself. After all, no one ever hated their own body, but they feed and care for their body, just as Christ does the church—for we are members of his body. "For this reason a man will leave his father and mother and be united to his wife, and the two will become one flesh." This is a profound mystery—but I am talking about Christ and the church. However, each one of you also must love his wife as he loves himself, and the wife must respect her husband.

Because Jim loved Aurora more than himself, he is able to claim the title of husband: he earned it. Forget the expensive wedding, forget the expensive ring; as a man, the only expense he needs to think about is sacrificing himself for his wife. This passage is misunderstood because people oftentimes only focus on the part of the passage, that reads, "submit yourselves to your husbands." God requires husbands to submit themselves just as much back to their wives if not more, because submitting means sacrificing.

*

Getting back to my problem with finding a job ... Eventually, I thought I struck gold. A girl who I had sent an encouraging quote to after she posted an embarrassing sales experience on LinkedIn reached out to me about a position at a large cloud computing company based out of California. The position would be based in north metro Atlanta and, in short, involved a lot of cold-calling. Having written several books that involved history, when they turned the tables and let me ask questions to them, I thought it would be natural to see who their favorite historical figure, were.

While it didn't go over well, judging from their answers and the passion they spoke with while they talked, deep down, I'm sure they appreciated it. Needless to say, however, I didn't get the position.

Still, I trudged on, sure a job would certainly come my way one day. In the hot July heat of Atlanta, I walked into a building that my Dad told me was prominent 30 years ago, but now was in need of a desperate makeover. When I arrived at the office, I made up my mind that the inside was much nicer and boasted a beautiful view, a view I could get used to. I felt at ease because the founders of the company were Buckhead dads, people I could really relate to. After interviewing with a few founders, my last was with the founder who found me on LinkedIn. I knew this because I saw that he had viewed my profile. He challenged me more than the others; later I realized this because I knew that he saw potential in me and knew that I could make him a lot of money. When he hired me, he told me I had the quickest turnaround time he had seen for someone to be hired in his 20-year career. When I started, I met the cadre of people I would soon work with. I also met someone who I had shockingly not met with before, considering he was to be my manager.[20]

To this day, I don't know if the founders *on purpose* didn't have me interview with the hiring manager because they might have known, in their heart of hearts, that he would have deemed me to be overqualified. Whatever the case was, from the outset, the manager felt threatened, and I don't blame him because on day two, I was already starting deals. We weren't supposed to be doing that

---

[20] In business, the *vast* majority of the time you interview with who is called your "hiring manger," whom you will ultimately report to.

for another month. He had reason to think I was dumb because I had trouble memorizing the "pitch" that we were supposed to memorize because of my learning difficulties.[21] He also felt threated because I was the oldest and had the most experience by far in technology sales. What made matters worse is that I was already an author. At one point, he quipped, "Thomas, you're always one step ahead of me, and I hate it when people are one step ahead of me!" I'm honestly surprised I lasted a week. At the company happy hour the night before I was fired, one of the more senior reps told me that the founder who had been hard on me because he knew I could produce "loved me."

On the last day of the week, Friday, the manager announced that there would be "performance reviews" given. I was to be first. When I walked into the room where I was to be reviewed, I noticed a slight problem: the HR representative was there. The manager told me I had trouble learning. When I told him that I had asserted myself as a great prospecter, which means to start deals, he insinuated that that particular job wasn't important even though a founder had asked the night before, "when are they hitting the phones?"

When he walked me out of the office, he was especially mean to me, almost as if he was rubbing it in my face that it was he who had the power over me. When I went back to my condo complex, I didn't know what to do; at the time, I didn't know why I was fired. There is no greater boon than to have a mentor who has your

---

[21] In actuality, there was no need to memorize this pitch because the vast majority of the work was done on the phone, and you could use notes while talking to somebody because they, of course, can't see you.

back during the most harrowing of times. For me, that mentor has been Nick Tzitzon[22]. When I told him what had happened, he simply said, "Look, most people are mediocre by nature. The second the 'new guy' threatens to expose the existing team by showing real star power, they retreat."

For me, I had nothing against the guy's decision. He had showed us a picture of one of his young kids, and in many ways he was protecting him/her because he knew that if I stayed on with the company and succeeded without his direction, I would eventually take his job. Ultimately, the founder's hands were tied because although I showed I could produce, they couldn't listen to someone who was there for only a week; they had to be loyal to their VP of Sales who had been there for years.

Looking for jobs was something I was used to doing, but I had never done so with such alacrity the week after I was fired. Honestly, I started that weekend, and for the next two weeks, I produced three job offers with competitors, and, had I kept interviewing, would have most likely produced more. Life is very reactionary; those who react with the most bravery during the most harrowing times are the ones who are remembered. In debates, politicians, by their debate coaches, are taught not to react in a negative way even if their competitors are trying to get under their skin. The reason for this is ultimately because the most impressive presidents of our day, from George Washington, to Abraham Lincoln, to FDR, to

---

[22] Tzitzon served as Executive Vice President at SAP under Bill McDermott from 2012 to 2019. He also was the head of Marketing and Communications for the company from 2017-19. He now is the Chief Strategy Officer at ServiceNow. Great leaders delegate.

Ronald Reagan, and Barack Obama have their greatness defined in moments where they reacted with bravery during the most challenging times. While debates are nothing like what a candidate will face as president, how people react to their opponents can set precedence on how they will react during the difficult, trying times while in office.

If anyone were going through harrowing times, it was Jim and Aurora, who were on the verge of sinking in a sinking ship. When Jim realized he is locked out of the door he needs to go into, he told Aurora that he'll have to stay there, which means that he will have to risk his life. Jim asked Aurora to open the door, and, when he does, she exclaimed, "No, you don't understand, if I open the If I open the door, it will kill you!"

The thing is, even though Aurora says he doesn't understand, the fact is he *does* understand; he understands the sacrifice he is making for the other 5000 passengers on the ship. Later, Aurora asks, "is this what you said was going to happen?" The question reminds me of Jesus predicting his own death, which he does three times in the Gospel of Matthew. In all three accounts, Jesus suffers for one reason: saving mankind from his sins. There is nothing more noble than to sacrifice oneself because in doing so, you are giving the power away to the other person instead of keeping it all yourself. The strongest mentors in my life have followed this way of thinking.

Later, when Jim tells Aurora that he is going to put himself in a precarious position, a position where he could potentially die, she tells him, "You die, I die!" It's the ultimate declaration of love, one that Peter could not do when he denied knowing Jesus. Matthew 26:33-35 reads,

> Peter replied, "Even if all fall away on account of you, I never will."
>
> "Truly I tell you," Jesus answered, "this very night, before the rooster crows, you will disown me three times."
>
> But Peter declared, "Even if I have to die with you, I will never disown you." And all the other disciples said the same.

By Aurora telling Jim that she must die if Jim were to die, she was telling him that she would not fall away on account of him. In *When You See It*[23], I say that "to start a relationship—whether it be romantic or simply friendship—there has to be a sense of permanence that will always be there. Without that, relationships cannot form properly—or at all." In the same vein, in *The Meaning of Marriage* by Tim Keller, he says "real love, the Bible says, instinctively desires permanence." To make something a permanent habit is taxing; it requires effort and there has to be some sacrifice there. In the more meaningful relationships I have had with people, sacrifice has been there; in the ones that have subsequently not mattered as much because there was no permanence there, sacrifice has not.

*

When Jim restores the ship, there is only one problem: his tether got detached from the ship, so he is left to float in space forever. Luckily, Aurora comes to the rescue, but once Jim is back on the ship, the infirmary pronounces him dead. While Aurora is rescuing Jim, I noticed something that I had not noticed during the

---

[23] Originally my 4th book to be released as my final book in 2025.

previous times I had watched the movie. One could say she is at her ugliest while rescuing Jim: she has blood all over her body, no makeup on, and is sweating profusely. Her speech is much more rapid because of all the adrenaline. It made me think that to make someone else beautiful, more often than not, we ourselves must become ugly. Since that's what Christ did for us, shouldn't we do the same in our relationships with others?

Jim does finally wake up, and the first thing he says is, "you brought me back." After Jim is brought back to life, he realizes, through a captain's ID, one person can go back into hibernation mode and sleep the next eighty years. Jim tells Aurora that she must be the one who goes. Before, by waking up Aurora, Jim chose comfort; now he chooses to suffer. His transformation reminds me of a verse in 1st Corinthians 13:11 that reads "When I was a child, I talked like a child, I thought like a child, I reasoned like a child. When I became a man, I set aside childish ways. Now we see but a dim reflection as in a mirror; then we shall see face to face. Now I know in part; then I shall know fully, even as I am fully known...." Naturally, we are going to think in a childish state growing up. The most successful of people let that childish state pass them by as fast as thoroughbred races on Kentucky spring day, running for 1st prize.

*

Aurora ends the movie by saying, "you can't get so hung up on where you'd rather be that you forget to make the most of where you are." Can you follow her direction? Do you have the courage to actually appreciate the suffering you're currently going through? Can you say, "I can?"

7

Cherishing What You Despise

The nineties were full of one-hit wonders from a music perspective. Some songs that come to mind are "Closing Time" by Semisonic, "She's so High" by Tal Bachman, and "Breakfast at Tiffany's" by Deep Blue Something. No song, however, I would argue was as powerful as "Bitter-Sweet Symphony" by the Verve. Proof of that is the song was the background music that was in one of the more meaningful Nike commercials ever made. We will get to that later, but first, I encourage you, the reader, to hear what the lead singer, Richard Ashcroft, had to say to the crowd during a rendition of the song that was performed during a concert in Glastonbury in 2008. Before the band starts playing the song, he says, "It's a struggle. Life's a struggle. Monday morning may be a struggle for a lot of you working in a job that you despise, working for a boss that you despise." It's interesting to think about how what we despise oftentimes makes life better. Just the other day, the owner of my company was hard on me, encouraging me to produce more. At the time, that was the last thing I wanted to hear, especially because others at the company told me I had been doing well. Because of his encouragement, however, I was able to produce a significant lead with a large accounting company, which could result in considerable commissions owed to me.

I told you I would analyze the Nike commercial later, so here's my overarching analysis: the commercial encourages you to cherish the things in sports with which you despise. But first, for a little bit of background, if the Verve had their drothers, the song would have never been used for a commercial at all. The band's manager, Jazz Summers, quipped "The Verve are a rock band, and they don't think their music should be used to endorse things." But, the band had no choice because they didn't own the rights to the song because the song includes a snippet of the Andrew Oldham Orchestra's version of the Rolling Stones track "The Last Time." Because of this, ABKCO had the choice to hire a band to rerecord the song whether the Verve wanted this to happen or not. Since they didn't want this to happen, the band tried to lure just one advertiser to buy the rights to a song to persuade the others to go away. In the end, Nike won the battle, beating out Budweiser, Coca-Cola, and General Motors in the process.

Im strong and will werk hard.

In Phil Knight's *New York Times* Best-Seller, *Shoe Dog: A Memoir by the Creator of Nike*, he states what I think my overarching analysis of the commercial is: "The cowards never started and the weak died along the way. That leaves us, ladies and gentlemen. Us." The name of the commercial is fittingly called, "I can." The opening ten seconds of the commercial reads, "I can play," but seconds later, it challenges the viewer because the following word appears on the screen: *anywhere*.

In one of the most ironic classics ever written, *Flowers for*

Algernon by Daniel Keyes, irony never ceases to occur. The main character is a retarded boy named Charlie Gordon. He is chosen for an experiment by a college hospital that is supposed to make him become a genius, thus making his worries and problems go away. One of the strongest quotes throughout the whole book is in the beginning when he knows what his goal is and how to achieve it. He tells himself, "Im strong and will werk hard." In our faith, that's absolutely true, for Isaiah 40:31 says, "But those who hope in the Lord will renew their strength. They will soar on wings like eagles; they will run and not grow weary, they will walk and not be faint."

Later in the commercial, there is a video of pee-wee football players where the running-back is forcefully running away from the defender, with the defender still holding on. Fittingly, while this this is happening, the words on the screen read, "I can hang on for dear life." We spoke of Job early in Chapter 1; now I'll analyze another test that he goes through in Job 2:1-10:

On another day the angels came to present themselves before the Lord, and Satan also came with them to present himself before him. And the Lord said to Satan, "Where have you come from?"

Satan answered the Lord, "From roaming throughout the earth, going back and forth on it."

Then the Lord said to Satan, "Have you considered my servant Job? There is no one on earth like him; he is blameless and upright, a man who fears God and shuns evil. And he still maintains his integrity, though you incited me against him to ruin him without any reason."

"Skin for skin!" Satan replied. "A man will give all he has for his own life. But now stretch out your hand and strike his flesh and bones, and he will surely curse you to your face."

The Lord said to Satan, "Very well, then, he is in your hands; but you must spare his life."

So Satan went out from the presence of the Lord and afflicted Job with painful sores from the soles of his feet to the crown of his head. Then Job took a piece of broken pottery and scraped himself with it as he sat among the ashes.

His wife said to him, "Are you still maintaining your integrity? Curse God and die!"

He replied, "You are talking like a foolish woman. Shall we accept good from God, and not trouble?"

In all this, Job did not sin in what he said.

The song, "Live Your Life," by TI, featuring Rihana, came out in 2008 and rose to the number one spot on the *Billboard* Hot 100. Without wasting much time, TI encourages the listener that it's necessary to be appreciative of your life and to stop focusing on what you don't have so that you can be thankful for what you possess. Even Job's wife questioned why he still maintained his integrity and encouraged to curse God. But Job will have none of it, insisting that he stay true to God. We often speak of God's unconditional love for us, so, since God has loved us unconditionally, shouldn't we also love him unconditionally back?

In the foreword of a *Man's Search for Meaning*, Harold Kushner writes about Frankl's most famous insight: "Forces beyond your control can take away everything you possess except one thing, your freedom to choose how you will respond to the situation. You cannot control what happens to you in your life, but you can always control what you feel and do about what happens to you."

There was no more pronounced time when I felt this way than the day after I nearly took my own life. I was so depressed during that time that I did something I had never done before or have done since: I dined and dashed at Steak & Shake in the wee hours of the morning. I was not thinking coherently enough to pay. [24] My mother came over to my condo the next afternoon. Previously that day, I wrote some about suicide. I hope you've never been suicidal before, but if you have, I think it can be summed up best when, in his *New York Times* best-selling book, *A First Rate Madness*, Nassir Ghaemi tells the reader what one of his patients once said: "Depression is a terrifying experience, knowing that somebody is going to kill you, and that person is *you*."

When I was in that restaurant, a strange thing happened. I

---

[24] I remembered what I did the next day and ended up paying that day.

felt as close to God as I had possibly ever felt before because I had a strange thought that didn't make any sense. The thought was directed at God and it was to thank God for my misery because I had remembered reading in Ghaemi's book a year earlier that when you go through intense pain, it expands the capacity to have greater empathy. I knew that I would treat people better in the long run because of what I was going through. I didn't like the pain, but I realized I had to sacrifice myself, and, as I say in *Forget Self-Help*, "you only love someone when you are willing to sacrifice for them; without sacrifice, there is no love."

As Joshua Wolf Shenk explains in *Lincoln's Melancholy*, during a deep depression, just as Abraham Lincoln instructed his best friend Joshua Speed to take away all the razors and anything Lincoln could use to kill himself. I, too, instructed my best friend Carson Pyles to take away all my medicine from me. I didn't wish to take any chances.

That Picture

Next, in the commercial, a runner comes onto the screen. To say that she is not happy would be quite the understatement. She is grimacing, ready to give up, but in that moment of inner turmoil and suffering, she provides peace to the viewer as well as strength because if she can do it, so can the viewer of the commercial. When I was in the first phase of Skyland Trail, a mental illness rehabilitation facility, ironically, for forty days and forty nights, I had pictures up on a board of family and friends. No picture was more meaningful than the picture of my brother completing a triathlon. Ripped, toned, and tan, it was more the look of determination on his face that taught me to get over the situation I now faced; I had to be strong like him.

Determination is necessary to advance, and, to advance at a meaningful rate, one in which we have the potential to accomplish something truly spectacular, we must first suffer in order to achieve our goal. The next clip of the commercial shows a young teenage girl shooting a free-throw. A free throw in basketball is when a player shoots a shot unguarded from 15 feet after he/she is fouled. She shoots the free-throw, and misses, causing her to be in complete dismay. It was the type of look that made you think instead of going out to a girls sleepover that night, she was going to first unlock the gym door, turn on the lights, and then spend the next two hours shooting free-throws until she improved her form, thus advancing her chances of making the next pivotal free throw in her next game.

In *Flowers for Algernon*, Charlie's occupation is to work at a bakery. Because he's retarded, he can't do much. The owner, Mr. Donner, keeps him on because of a promise he made to his parents. After his operation, however, Mr. Donner sees that Charlie can become quite useful, in fact. Charlie learns how to use the mixer, even though it took someone else two years to learn how to do it, and they had gone to bakery school. Below, Charlie explains how it felt to *advance*.

Everybody was crowded around and talking about it and I got scared because they all looked at me funny and they were excited. Frank said I told you there is something peculiar lately about Charlie. And Joe Carp says yeah I know what you mean. Mr Donner sent everybody back to work and he took me out to the front of the store with him.

He said Charlie I dont know how you done it but it looks like you finally learned something. I want you to be carefull and do the best you can do. You got yourself a new job with a 5 dollar raise.

I said I dont want a new job because I like to clean up and sweep and deliver and do things for my friends but Mr Donner said never mind your friends I need you for this job. I dont think much of a man who dont want to advance.

I said whats advance mean. He scratched his head and looked at me over his glasses. Never mind that Charlie. From now on you work that mixer. Thats advance.

So now instead of delivering packiges and washing out the toliets and dumping the garbage. In the new mixer. That's advance. Tomorrow I will tell Miss Kinnian. I think she will be happy but I dont know why Frank and Joe are mad at me. I asked Fanny and she said never mind those fools. This is April Fools day and the joke backfired and made them the fools instead of you.

I asked Joe to tell me what was the joke that back-fired and he said go jump in the lake. I guess their mad at me because I worked the mashine but they didn't get the day off like they thought. Does that mean I'm getting smarter.

I, too, felt like Charlie before I published my first book and after it was deemed that I had become a successful writer. Some friends made fun of me before the first book got published, and, not surprisingly, they were the people that never showed an appreciation for my writing after I had success.

Real Courage

Later on, in *To Kill a Mockingbird*, in speaking of Mrs. Dubose, Atticus explains to Jem what exactly real courage meant when you do in fact suffer.

She was a great lady... She was. She had her own views about things, a lot different from mine, maybe... son, I told you that if you hadn't lost your head I'd have made you go read to her. I wanted you to see something about her- I wanted you to see what real courage is, instead of getting the idea that courage is a man with a gun in his hand. It's when you know you're licked before you begin but you begin anyway and you see it through no matter what. You rarely win, but sometimes you do. Mrs. Dubose won, all ninety-eight pounds of her. According to her views, she died beholden to nothing and nobody. She was the bravest person I ever knew.

Once again, in *The Road to Character*, by David Brooks, he states "when most people think about the future, they dream up ways they might live happier lives. But notice this phenomenon. When people remember the crucial events that formed them, they don't usually talk about happiness. It is usually the ordeals that seem most significant. Most people shoot for happiness but feel formed through suffering."

Ultimately, God knew that the most unpleasant part of human life was to suffer. This is why he came down in the flesh in the form of Jesus Christ. Christ knew that to suffer on another's behalf was the only way to get to truly know someone. In His suffering on the cross, we were formed.

*

Next, in the commercial, we see a clip of Mia Hamm, former stand-out U.S. soccer star, heading a ball into the net for a goal. She tells the camera, "I can be anything; I can do anything on the field." Once you find that special place—where you can do anything—never leave it, for if you do, your soul will go too. For me, that special place has become the paper with which I write on; many of my friends have been surprised by the way I write because I do not speak nearly as well, only when I am comfortable with the person I am talking to or passionate about the subject matter do I come across as intelligent. Scoring a goal is to Mia Hamm what a positive media review is to me; both rejuvenate us and make us come back for more.

When you're ready to come back for more, just know that it often means more suffering. Are you brave enough to handle it? During my favorite part of the commercial, there are men running, and a caption that says, "I can run with my dog." Then, it is almost as if the runner feels a second-wind because he says, "I can get a *faster* dog (italics added). Can you say, like Kevin Bacon did in *Animal House* while he is getting paddled in a fraternity ritual, "Thank you sir, may I have another?" Many people not only dislike pain but stay as far away from it as they can. The few who embrace it know that by staying away from it, they will never get to the point where they will say, "I can."

More Than Conquerors

Embracing pain is the first step in conquering your fear, which is what pops up on the screen next. In one of the most quoted passages in the Bible of all time, Paul writes:

> And we know that in all things God works for the good of those who love him, who have been called according to his purpose. For those God foreknew he also predestined to be conformed to the image of his Son, that he might be the firstborn among many brothers and sisters. And those he predestined, he also called; those he called, he also justified; those he justified, he also glorified.

> What, then, shall we say in response to these things? If God is for us, who can be against us? He who did not spare his own Son, but gave him up for us all—how will he not also, along with him, graciously give us all things? Who will bring any charge against those whom God has chosen? It is God who justifies. Who then is the one who condemns? No one. Christ Jesus who died—more than that, who was raised to life—is at the right hand of God and is also interceding for us. Who shall separate us from the love of Christ? Shall trouble or hardship or persecution or famine or nakedness or danger or sword? As it is

written:

"For your sake we face death all day long; we are considered as sheep to be slaughtered."

No, in all these things we are more than conquerors through him who loved us. For I am convinced that neither death nor life, neither angels nor demons, neither the present nor the future, nor any powers, neither height nor depth, nor anything else in all creation, will be able to separate us from the love of God that is in Christ Jesus our Lord. (Romans 8:28-39)

Verse thirty-five says, "Who shall separate us from the love of Christ? Shall trouble or hardship or persecution or famine or nakedness or danger or sword?" Later, verse thirty-seven answers this question: "no, in all these things we are more than conquerors through him who loved us." When you have nothing to fear, you can dance in the type of way you would as if no one's watching, you can sing as if you were in the shower, but most importantly, you can be free, free from judgment or concern. It's only freeing to be free because all our sins have been paid for by Jesus on the cross.

In 1932, in the middle of the Great Depression, FDR knew that Americans had fears, and he was the person that must resolve them.

I am certain that my fellow Americans expect that on my induction into the Presidency I will address them with a candor and a decision which the present situation of our people impel. This is preeminently the time to speak the truth, the whole truth, frankly and boldly. Nor need we shrink from honestly facing conditions in our country today. This great Nation will endure as it has endured, will revive and will prosper. So, first of all, let me assert my firm belief that the only thing we have to fear is fear itself—nameless, unreasoning, unjustified terror which paralyzes needed efforts to convert retreat into advance. In every dark hour of our national life a leadership of frankness and vigor has met with that understanding and support of the people themselves which is essential to victory. I am convinced that you will again give that support to leadership in these critical days.

The word advance—which we talked about earlier in this chapter—is what stands out most in his entire speech. So often, we fail to advance in our moments of suffering and instead, retreat. Vigor is another word that stands out. More often than not, we're used to hearing the word vigorous because it is a word that describes action, while vigor alone represents action. Either way you use the word, action is involved, which is fitting because the only way to get through suffering is action—vigorous action.

At the beginning of the commercial, there is a young girl who first smiles at the camera, then laughs. She is the youngest human being in the commercial. Fittingly, the commercial ends with an older man—the oldest human-being in the commercial. Throughout life, we all suffer, but we all also have the choice as to how we will respond. As the older man is running up the stadium stairs, the caption "I can" comes onto the screen with every step. Just as he can, so, too, can you, for to choose to suffer is not to retreat, but to advance.

Author's Note

"I have said what I wanted to say, and I will not say it again." – Harper Lee

@ Ellen: I hereby challenge you to a dance-off on your show.

@ Keith: I hope you invite me to speak at Faculty Forum one day in August.

To the parking lot attendant who I was mean to when I didn't have cash or a credit card to pay my parking fee after my trip down to Orlando with my Morehouse Sales Team: I am sorry.

To the front desk receptionist at the hotel in St. Paul: Sorry I cussed you out when you told me you could not take my family member's credit card number over the phone. I shouldn't have done that considering I was there for a book signing and my book dealt with living out the Golden Rule.

Both of these sins happened because I lost my credit card and didn't have cash to pay them. Because I have such bad ADD, I literally lose my credit card every six months. I talked about dining and dashing at Steak & Shake that night I was depressed in the last chapter of this book. The other day, I realized I accidentally stole three Cliff Bars from the CVS after I got my medication because I got distracted. Later, I went back and paid for them. If some girl ever tries to pick me up at the CVS on Westheimer Road in Houston by asking, "come here often?" I will emphatically respond with, "Yes, I do!"

@ USGA: I agree with most of the rule changes in 2019 except for the rule in which you are only allotted three minutes to look for your lost ball instead of the previous five. Unless Tiger Woods gives me lessons to improve my golf game, I am going to try get the rule changed back.

@ Justin Bieber: I'm impressed you have come out with 5 or 6 hits in the last 12 months. I will catch up to you, however. Your song, "Holy," featuring Chance The Rapper, is in my 7th book, *Alone at the Lunch Table: How to Rise From Rejection*. Thanks for inspiring me. Because you have inspired me, I will inspire others.

Epilogue (Realistic Fiction)

You're in town for a wedding for a friend you haven't seen in a few years. You almost considered not going to the wedding because you knew you wouldn't know anybody because the friend you met happened to be in the booth next door at a trade show several years back. You figured most of the people at the wedding would be college or high-school friends that you didn't know. I still felt obligated to go because this friend made that big of an impression on you even then. On multiple occasions, when he saw that the usual five-minute initial meet and greet with a prospect turned into a forty-five minute demo of my company's software, he would literally walk to the concession stand and buy *my* prospect a bottle of water. I kid you not, that personal touch helped me get two [25] PoC's with Fortune 500 companies and one of those deals eventually closed.

You met this friend five years ago, and you're awestruck at how personable[26] of a person he is. He is not only been there for me in situations like when I got laid off three years ago after my company got bought out[27], but he was the first one to congratulate me when I became the number one rep in the country at the current company

---

[25] Proof of Concept- (A Trial Run of the Software)
[26] "A person is a person through other persons." – Desmond Tutu
[27] I had a job within two months because he referred me to a former boss of his.

I am at. Rather than be jealous of my success, he seems energized by it.

So, I owed it to him to come to his wedding. Only one problem, though: inevitably, Google Maps only work 88% of the time. This is one of the 12% of the times where it doesn't work, and because the wedding is in a rural setting, I had to rent a car. I know, so 1997. Not to mention it's pouring down rain. Because it's pouring down rain, my flight got delayed two hours and by the time I get in the car to go to the rehearsal dinner, I realize that it already started forty-five minutes earlier. I'm stranded. I've got one option: give Bill a call.

He answers on the first ring. He immediately not only calms me down but explains in the simplest way possible how to get to the venue where the rehearsal dinner is. I get there in thirty minutes but miss all the toasts and speeches unfortunately. I soon forget that because prime-rib—cooked just the way I like it (medium rare)—and asparagus tend to do have this sort of effect on me.

*

The next day is fun. We play some golf (I'm snap hooking my driver throughout the round) and then we get ready for the wedding. At the rehearsal dinner, I spotted one of his fiancé's sorority sisters who was pretty cute. I told her—if I got up the nerve—I would ask her to dance the following evening. Luckily, I ended up having the courage to ask her dance. While we were dancing, we were talking—getting to know another. She spoke of her days with Julie, my friend's fiancé, and I tried to get her to laugh by my "it's so 1997 that I had to rent a car." When I told her that, she asked, "so you're the one who got lost last night?" I then asked her a question in response: "How'd you know?" She then said, "well, you interrupted Bill's speech at the rehearsal dinner."

*

In life, it is not so much about making the call, but taking the call.

David Brooks
"What Do You Say to the Sufferer?"
December 9th, 2021
The New York Times

Several weeks ago, I gave a talk, and afterward the questions from the audience came to me on index cards. Most of the questions were about politics or society, but one card read: "What do you do when you've spent your life wanting to be dead?"

I didn't answer that card because I didn't know anything about the person who wrote it, and because I didn't know what to say. But it has haunted me and I've kept the card on my night stand ever since.

I wish I'd said that I don't have any answers for you, but I do have a response. My response would start with the only things I know about you: You've been through a lot of pain over the course of your life. You have amazing powers of endurance because you are still here. I know you're fighting still because you reached out to me. My response begins with deep respect for you.

The other thing I know is that you are not alone. There is always a lot of suffering in the world, and over the past few years we have seen high tides of despair. The sources of people's pain may be different — grief, shame, exclusion, heartbreak, physical or mental health issues — but they almost always involve some feeling of isolation, of being cut off from others.

In my own seasons of suffering, I've been shocked at how emotional pain feels like searing physical pain in the stomach and chest, by how tempting it is to self-isolate and rob yourself of the very human contact you need most. But when it comes to extreme suffering, I must look to people who know more about it than I do, and one of those people is Viktor Frankl, who survived the Nazi death camps.

Frankl argued that we often can't control what happens to us in life, that we can control only how we respond to it. If we respond to terrible circumstances with tenacity, courage, unselfishness and dignity, then we can add a deeper meaning to life. One can win small daily victories over hard circumstances.

There were many people in the camps who wanted to die more than live. In "Man's Search for Meaning," Frankl wrote that he would try to help them recognize that "life was still expecting something from them; something in the future was expected of them." Frankl liked to paraphrase Nietzsche: "He who has a why to live for can bear with almost any how."

The Bible is filled with characters who are at times overwhelmed with life and wish they could be rid of it — Jonah, Elijah, Job and even Moses. They are so central to the biblical story because desolation is part of the human experience, part of the bricks and mortar out of which we construct our lives.

Suffering had such profound and unpredictable effects on those characters, as it does on all of us. Suffering can make people self-centered, loveless, humorless and angry. But we all know cases where suffering didn't break people but broke them open — made them more caring toward and knowledgeable about the suffering of others. And the old saying that we suffer our way to wisdom is not wrong. We often learn more from the hard times than the happy ones.

And so we are right to treat those who have suffered with respect and credibility. "Without your wound where would your power be?" Thornton Wilder wrote. "It is your very remorse that makes your low voice tremble into the hearts of men. The very angels themselves cannot persuade the wretched and blundering children on earth as can one human being broken on the wheels of living. In love's service only the wounded soldiers can serve."

This doesn't mean that those who have suffered should go out giving sermons and lectures. We all know the weakness of words in these circumstances. But having tasted desolation, those who have suffered do powerfully sit with others in their desolation.

Rabbi Elliot Kukla once described a woman with a brain injury who would sometimes fall to the floor. People around her would rush to immediately get her back on her feet, before she was quite ready. She told Kukla, "I think people rush to help me up because they are so uncomfortable with seeing an adult lying on the floor. But what I really need is for someone to get down on the ground with me."

Kukla pointed out that getting on the floor can be anxiety-producing and, when someone is in deep despair, even dangerous to the strongest caregiver. But sometimes you just get on the floor.

We all need witnesses — to witness others, to be witnessed, to draw inspiration from each other. "Consolation is an act of solidarity in space," Michael Ignatieff wrote in his new book, "On Consolation."

I asked a pastor what he says to people in pain. One thing he says is, "I want more for you." I repeat that sentence to you not with any illusion that the world does what I want, but simply as an expression of good will, an acknowledgment of how we all sit with our common fragility, and a recognition that life is unpredictable. It changes. In many pilgrims' progress, the slough of despond gives way to enchanted ground.

If you are having thoughts of suicide, in the United States call the National Suicide Prevention Lifeline at 800-273-8255 (TALK) or go to SpeakingOfSuicide.com/resources for a list of additional resources. Go here for resources outside the United States.

Excerpt from *A First-Rate Madness: Uncovering the Links Between Mental Illness and Leadership*

DEPRESSION DEEPENS our natural empathy, and produces someone for whom the inescapable web of interdependence (one of Martin Luther King's phrases) is a personal reality, not a fanciful wish. Depression cultivates empathic experience, ripens it, until, in a select few, it blooms into exemplary abilities.

Thus arises the empathic leader, a person sometimes so arresting that the rest of us become convinced he must be an otherworldly saint, a uniquely great soul, an anomalous event. He may be all those—but perhaps his secret is more prosaic: the common yet profound imprint of depression.

Mahatma Gandhi and Martin Luther King are the bookends of depressive activism, the innovators of a new politics of radical empathy that didn't exist before Gandhi and hasn't persisted after King. Though their countries and the world remain deeply influenced by their legacies, neither India nor the United States could now be said to exemplify the nonviolent ideals of these men. Their politics of radical empathy could not be maintained by leaders who lacked their vision—and their illness. They both attempted suicide

130

as teenagers, endured at least one depressive episode in midlife, and suffered a very severe depressive episode in their final years, before they were killed. They each pushed the politics of empathy to its limits, and found their followers—the mass of normal human-kind—unable to keep up with them.

Each man is now sanctified in the public mind, but few of us really appreciate them for who they were, for their weaknesses as well as their strengths, for the rejection they faced during their lives, and the depression they repeatedly endured and—in their empathy for others' suffering—ultimately overcame.

References

Chapter 1

1. American Express Rain "Rain" (Tiger Woods.) https://www.youtube.com/watch?v=UVDpurEhHiQ. May 19th, 2014. Retrieved March 6th 2021.

2. American Express Tiger Woods Rainy Day. https://www.youtube.com/watch?v=Vc9afbahGHw. September 11th, 2013. Retrieved March 6th 2021.

3. "Golf: How Tiger Woods finally managed to changed his stripes." Donaldson, Michael. NZ Herald. https://www.nzherald.co.nz/sport/golf-how-tiger-woods-finally-managed-to-change-stripes/EXSYZ5Q4QBIMXYBPCFYCYPPORQ/. April 19th 2019. March 6th 2021.

4. "Masters 2019: Tiger Woods's fellow Tour pros watched his victory with a mix of awe and admiration." Shipnuck, Alan. Golf Magazine. https://golf.com/news/tournaments/masters-2019-tiger-woods-victory-hailed-peers/. April 15th 2019. March 6th 2021.

5. "These Difficulties ... rather animate me than daunt me" James Oglethorpe as a Leader. Juile Anne Sweet. The Georgia Historical Quarterly. Vol. 99. Georgia Historical Quarterly. https://www.jstor.org/stable/44735574?seq=1. Page 148.

6. *Robert E. Lee: A Biography.* Emory Thomas. Page 152. Norton. New York. 1995.

7. *Holy Bible.* Page 1126. Zondevan. NIV. 1986.

8. "Fighter." *Merriam-Webster.com Dictionary*, Merriam-Webster, https://www.merriam-webster.com/dictionary/fighter. Accessed

6 Mar. 2021.

9.   "Bigger Than My Body." John Mayer. https://genius.com/John-mayer-bigger-than-my-body-lyrics.   Retrieved March 6th, 2021.

10. *Holy Bible*. Page 788. Zondevan. NIV. 1986.

11. *Holy Bible*. Page 789. Zondervan. NIV. 1986.

Chapter 2

1.   *To Kill a Mockingbird*. Harper Lee. Grand Central Publishing. New York. 2010. Page 142.

2.   *Holy Bible*. Exodus 1:11. Page 88. Zondervan. NIV. 1986.

3.   "Why Addictions Are So Hard to Break." Jennifer Kurnst. August 15th, 2012. Psychology Today. https://www.psychologytoday.com/us/blog/headshrinkers-guide-the-galaxy/201208/why-addictions-are-so-hard-break. Retrieved March 6th, 2021.

4.   "Fighter." Christina Aguilera. https://genius.com/Christina-aguilera-fighter-lyrics. Retrieved March 6th, 2021.

5.   *Holy Bible*. Page 864-5. Zondevan. NIV. 1986.

6.   *The Criminal: The Power of an Apology*. Thomas Fellows. Page 4. Yawn's Publishing. 2020.

7.   *To Kill a Mockingbird*. Harper Lee. Grand Central Publishing. New York. 2010. Page 142.

8.   *Holy Bible*. Exodus 14:10-14. Page 88. Zondervan. NIV. 1986.

9.   *The Crisis: No. 1*. Thomas Paine. 1776.

10. "National Flag in US: Quotes To Share With Family Friends on This Auspicious Day." Republicworld.com.

11. https://www.republicworld.com/lifestyle/festivals/na-

tional-flag-day-quotes.html. Riddhi Adsul. June 14th, 2020. Retrieved March 6th, 2021.

12.   *To Kill a Mockingbird*. Harper Lee. Grand Central Publishing. New York. 2010. Page 147-8.

13.   "Thoughts on the Business of Life." Forbes. Forbes Quotes. https://www.forbes.com/quotes/9319/. Retrieved March 7, 2021.

14.   *Holy Bible*. Isaiah 41:10. Page 1122. Zondervan. NIV. 1986.

15.   "Multiple sclerosis." Mayo Clinic. https://www.mayo-clinic.org/diseases-conditions/multiple-sclerosis/symptoms-causes/syc-20350269. Retrieved March 7th 2021.

16.   "Mercy." Dave Matthews Band. https://genius.com/Dave-matthews-band-mercy-lyrics. Retrieved March 7th, 2021.

17.   *Uncle Tom's Cabin*. Harriet Beecher Stowe. Page 262. The Modern Library. New York. 2000.

18.   "Plight." Lexico. https://www.lexico.com/definition/plight. Retrieved March 7th, 2021.

Chapter 3

1.   "Celebrating Dr. Martin Luther King Jr: Letters from a Birmingham Jail. Ed Stetzer. Christianity Today. https://www.christianitytoday.com/edstetzer/2020/january/letters-from-birmingham-jail.html. January 18th, 2021. Retrieved March 7th, 2021.

2.   *Holy Bible*. Acts 8:1-3 Page 1122. Zondervan. NIV. 1986.

3.   *Lord of the Flies*. William Golding. Page 11. Penguin. New York. 2016.

4.   Carl Sandburg's *Abraham Lincoln: The War Years*, Volume IV, p. 146.

5.   *Holy Bible.* Luke 2:33-35. Page 1122. Zondervan. NIV. 1986.

6.   "Richard Jewell." Strathcona County Library. https://scl.biblio-com'ons.com/item/ugc/2833479053?ugc_id=1717491249. Retrieved March 7th, 2021.

7.   "Raymond J. de Souza: 'We must not be enemies' : Lessons from Lincoln and the holder of his: Lincoln and Douglas established that the Union would be preserved not only by force of arms, but by, as much as possible, a unifying spirit." Father Raymond J. de Souza. National Post. https://nationalpost.com/opinion/raymond-j-de-souza-we-must-not-be-enemies-lessons-from-lincoln-and-the-holder-of-his-hat. March 4th, 2021. Retrieved March 7th, 2021.

8.   *A First-Rate Madness: Uncovering the Links Between Leadership and Mental Illness.* Nassir Ghaemi. Penguin. 2011.

9.   *Lincoln's Melancholy.* Joshua Wolf Shenk. Page 29. Mariner Books. 2006.

10.   Douglas L. Wilson and Rodney O. Davis, *Herndon's Informants: Letters, Interviews, and Statements about Abraham Lincoln,* p. 590 (Letter from Joshua F. Speed to William H. Herndon, ca 1882).

Chapter 4

1.   *The Road to Character.* David Brooks. Page 93. Random House. New York. 2015.

2.   *Holy Bible.* Matthew 26:36-46. Page 1544. Zondervan. NIV. 1986.

3. *The Road to Character.* David Brooks. Page 95-96. Random House. New York. 2015.
4. "Rocky 1976." https://www.quotes.net/mquote/1198685. Retrieved March 7th, 2021.
5. "Roberto Goizueta Quotes." http://www.quoteswise.com/roberto-goizueta-quotes-2.html. Retrieved March 7th, 2021.
6. *The Road to Character.* David Brooks. Random House. New York. 2015.
7. "The Founder – Persistence Speech." https://www.youtube.com/watch?v=oaStAR7hz_s. April 7th, 2017. Retrieved March 9th, 2021.
8. *Forget Self-Help: Re-Examining the Golden Rule.* Thomas Fellows. Page 6. Yawn's Publishing. 2017.
9. *A First-Rate Madness: Uncovering the Links Between Leadership and Mental Illness.* Page 256. Nassir Ghaemi. Penguin. 2011.

Chapter 5

1. *The Formative Years: At Atlanta's Westminster Schools.* William L. Pressly. McGuire Publishing. Page 92.
2. *A First-Rate Madness: Uncovering the Links Between Leadership and Mental Illness.* Page 56. Nassir Ghaemi. Penguin. 2011.
3. *Winners Dream: A Journey from the Corner Store to the Corner Office.* Bill McDermont. Simon & Shuster. New York. 2014.
4. *A Man's Search for Meaning.* Viktor E. Frankl. Beacon. Boston. 2006.
5. *Winners Dream: A Journey from the Corner Store to the Corner Office.* Page 15. Bill McDermont. Simon & Shuster. New York. 2014.

6.   "What would happen if the Earth stopped spinning?" Dr. Sten   Odenwald.   https://image.gsfc.nasa.gov/poetry/ask/q1168.html. 1997. Retrieved March 12th, 2021.

7.   *Holy Bible*. Romans 5:3-5. Page 1752. Zondervan. NIV. 1986.

8.   *Lincoln's Melancholy: How Depression Challenged a President and Fueled His Greatness*. Joshua Wolf Shenk. Mariner Books. New York. 2006.

9.   *Winners Dream: A Journey from the Corner Store to the Corner Office*. Page 22. Bill McDermont. Simon & Shuster. New York. 2014.

10.   *Holy Bible*. 1st Timothy 6:10. Page 1752. Zondervan. NIV. 1986.

11.   *Holy Bible*. Matthew 25:14-30. Page 1541. Zondervan. NIV. 1986.

12.   *Winners Dream: A Journey from the Corner Store to the Corner Office*. Bill McDermont. Simon & Shuster. New York. 2014.

Chapter 6

1.   "Mokokoma Mokhonaoana Quotes" https://www.goodreads.com/quotes/7697292-when-you-are-unemployed-weekends-are-seven-days-long. Retrieved March 13th, 2021.

2.   "Adam Smith on What it Means to Flourish." Ryan Patrick Hanley. Foundation for Economic Education. https://fee.org/articles/adam-smith-on-what-it-means-to-flourish/.   October   5th, 2016. Retrieved March 13th, 2021.

3.   "Passengers."   https://www.imdb.com/title/tt1355644/characters/nm0790688. Retrieved March 13th, 2021.

4.   "Nepotism."   Dictionary.com.   https://www.diction-ary.com/browse/nepotism. Retrieved March 13th, 2021.

5.   "Lost in Space."   The Media Tourist.   https://neilsenter-tainmentpicks.com/2016/12/27/lost-in-space/.   December 27th, 2016. Retrieved March 13th, 2021.

6.   *Forget Self-Help: Re-Examining the Golden Rule.* Thomas Fellows. Page 8 and 66. Yawn's Publishing. 2017.

7.   "To Build a Fire."   Jack London. Page 64 and 65. https://americanenglish.state.gov/files/ae/resource_files/to-build-a-fire.pdf. Retrieved March 13th, 2021.

8.   "To Build a Fire."   Jack London. Page 72. https://americanenglish.state.gov/files/ae/resource_files/to-build-a-fire.pdf. Retrieved March 13th, 2021.

9.   "Warehouse."   Dave   Matthews   Band.   https://genius.com/Dave-matthews-band-warehouse-lyrics. Retrieved March 13th, 2021.

10.   "How to Survive a Rip Current: First, Don't Fight It." Maggie   Astor.   *The   New   York   Times.*   https://www.nytimes.com/2017/07/31/us/riptide-rip-current-drowning-safety.html. July 31st, 2017. Retrieved March 13th, 2021.

11.   *A First-Rate Madness: Uncovering the Links Between Leadership and Mental Illness.* Page 46. Nassir Ghaemi. Penguin. 2011.

12.   *Holy Bible.* Romans 12:2. Page 1763. Zondervan. NIV. 1986.

13.   *Holy Bible.* Matthew 5:11. Page 1501. Zondervan. NIV. 1986.

14.   "Passengers."   https://english-from-movies.weebly.com/uploads/5/0/2/2/5022041/passengers.txt. . Retrieved March 13th, 2021.

15.   "Passengers."   https://english-from-movies.wee-
bly.com/uploads/5/0/2/2/5022041/passengers.txt. . Retrieved
March 13th, 2021.
16.   "A Modell for Christian Charity." John Winthrop.
https://liberalarts.utexas.edu/coretexts/_files/re-
sources/texts/1630%20Model%20of%20Christian%20Char-
ity.pdf. April 8th, 1630. Retrieved March 13th, 2021.
17.   "Movie Review: Passengers (Chris Pratt & Jennifer Law-
rence.) Conservative Book Club. https://www.conservative-
bookclub.com/22943/featured-article/movie-review-passengers-
chris-pratt-jennifer-lawrence.
18.   "To Build a Fire." Jack London. Page 76. https://ameri-
canenglish.state.gov/files/ae/resource_files/to-build-a-fire.pdf.
Retrieved March 13th, 2021.
19.   "Passengers."   https://english-from-movies.wee-
bly.com/uploads/5/0/2/2/5022041/passengers.txt. . Retrieved
March 13th, 2021.
20.   "If." Rudyard Kipling. https://www.poetryfounda-
tion.org/poems/46473/if---. . Retrieved March 13th, 2021.
21.   "Robert E. Lee." Kappa Alpha Order. https://www.kap-
paalphaorder.org/ka/history/lee/. Retrieved March 13th, 2021.
22.   *Holy Bible.* Ephesians 5:22-33. Page 1823. Zondervan. NIV.
1986.
23.   "Passengers."   https://english-from-movies.wee-
bly.com/uploads/5/0/2/2/5022041/passengers.txt. . Retrieved
March 13th, 2021.
24.   *Holy Bible.* Matthew 26:33-35. Page 1544. Zondervan. NIV.
1986.
25.   *When You See It.* Thomas Fellows.
26.   *The Meaning of Marriage.* Tim Keller. Hodder & Stoughton.

2011.

27.   "Passengers."   https://english-from-movies.wee-bly.com/uploads/5/0/2/2/5022041/passengers.txt. .   Retrieved March 13th, 2021.

28.   *Holy Bible.* 1st Corinthians 13:11. Page 1787. Zondervan. NIV. 1986.

29.   "Passengers."   https://english-from-movies.wee-bly.com/uploads/5/0/2/2/5022041/passengers.txt. .   Retrieved March 13th, 2021.

Chapter 7

1.   "♥ ♫ ♪ The Verve: Bitter Sweet Symphony "live", Glastonbury   2008   HD   ♥   ♫   ♪   AWESOME." https://www.youtube.com/watch?v=WdD-kborQRU. September 22nd, 2010. Retrieved March 13th, 2021.

2.   "Infamous Nike commercial." https://www.theverve-live.com/2008/05/infamous-nike-commer-cial.html#:~:text=%22The%20Verve%20are%20a%20rock%20band,%20and%20they,not%20control%20publish-ing%20rights%20to%20%22Bitter%20Sweet%20Symphony.%22. May 1st, 2008. Retrieved March 13th, 2021.

3.   *Shoe Dog: A Memoir by the Creator of Nike.* Phil Knight. Scribner. New York. 2016.

4.   *Flowers for Algernon.* Daniel Keyes. Page 4. Mariner. New York.

5.   *Holy Bible.* Isaiah 41:31. Page 1121. Zondervan. NIV. 1986.

6.   *Holy Bible.* Job 2:1-10. Page 790. Zondervan. NIV. 1986.

7.   "Live Your Life." T.I. Featuring Rihanna. https://ge-nius.com/Ti-live-your-life-lyrics. Retrieved March 13th, 2021.

8. *A Man's Search for Meaning.* Page X. Viktor E. Frankl. Beacon. Boston. 2006.

9. *A First-Rate Madness: Uncovering the Links Between Leadership and Mental Illness.* Page 12. Nassir Ghaemi. Penguin. 2011.

10. *Forget Self-Help: Re-Examining the Golden Rule.* Thomas Fellows. Page 8. Yawn's Publishing. 2017.

11. *Flowers for Algernon.* Daniel Keyes. Page 35-36. Mariner. New York.

12. *To Kill a Mockingbird.* Harper Lee. Grand Central Publishing. New York. 2010. Page 147-8.

13. *To Kill a Mockingbird.* Harper Lee. Grand Central Publishing. New York. 2010. Page 149.

14. *The Road to Character.* David Brooks. Page 93. Random House. New York. 2015.

15. "Nike - I – Can Commercial." https://www.youtube.com/watch?v=8FqKRN5FQgw Retrieved March 13th, 2021.

16. "Thank you sir, may I have another?" Richard Baehr. American Thinker. February 8th, 2005. https://www.americanthinker.com/articles/2005/02/thank_you_sir_may_i_have_anoth.html, Retrieved March 13th, 2021.

17. *Holy Bible.* Romans 8:28-39 Page 1757-58. Zondervan. NIV. 1986.

18. "Inaugural Address – March 04, 1933." The American Presidency Project." https://www.presidency.ucsb.edu/documents/inaugural-address-8. Retrieved March 13th, 2021.

From the Pages of *Forget Self-Help: Re-Examining the Golden Rule*

Nonetheless, when someone bears our burdens with us, often a huge weight lifts from our shoulders. Does this mean that the other person can solve the problem that the other one is going through? *No.* However, just knowing that someone cares enough to forget his *own* problems and focus on *yours* is reassuring.
—CHAPTER 1

When people speak of having an advantage over someone, they often feel as if they have to tread on sharp glass. There is no need to do this because none of us created our own advantages. They were given to us by God. However, we do need to tread lightly on how we use our own advantages to help others.   **—CHAPTER 2**

Usually, when we ourselves are in a position of power, we like to look to see how we can use it to control others instead of realizing that we need to control ourselves that much more because of the position we are now in.   **—CHAPTER 2**

A man's heart is only strong when it is safe, and it is only safe when it is secured in something strong.   **—CHAPTER 2**

Since none of us will see God on Earth, we face an uphill battle to show others that God truly exists.   **—CHAPTER 3**

One reason that we never get to know other people is because it requires us to become vulnerable to other people. To become vulnerable not only requires work but also requires courage. Many people are unwilling to admit their blind spots or flaws. However, when this happens, a whole new world is opened up because it enables both parties to be real with each other.   **—CHAPTER 4**

Without loving oneself first, it is impossible to love others.
—CHAPTER 4

Everyone can agree though that anything worthwhile, anything worth striving for, has some element of rarity to it. **—CHAPTER 5**

When judging another person, I never look for the big moments that test their character. I look for the small ones. Big moments carry a heroic aspect to them so there is a certain selfish incentive to make sure they are carried out to fruition. Small moments, however, never get any credit. This accentuates their value. **—CHAPTER 6**

We need to be extreme. We need to be bold. We need to go all out. But we need to do this all for others, not ourselves. **—CHAPTER 6**

The best way to tell if someone is with you is to see whether a person will help you even if he knows he will get nothing in return from you. Anyone can help when there is something to gain in return; to help when there is nothing to be gained shows true love. **—CHAPTER 7**

Showing mercy toward others is not an easy task. It requires patience, humility, and an inverse style of thinking that goes against our natural selfish desires. It also requires giving up a sense of control, a sense of control we often feel like we earned in the first place. —CHAPTER 7

Holding someone accountable for their actions can be one of the most delicate and awkward dealings that a human being has to do for another. But in strong relationships, this happens frequently. — **CHAPTER 8**

So many times, we lash out against others when they give us advice or critique our actions. We need to realize they are doing so because they believe in us and think we are capable of greatness. —**CHAPTER 8**

When we do for others, we provide more happiness for ourselves more effectively than when we try to focus only on ourselves. The reason for this is simple: putting ourselves in another's shoes makes us forget all about our own problems. —**CHAPTER 8**

What happens when we focus less on ourselves and instead devote that energy toward others? We benefit others and also benefit ourselves. When we reach out to someone who is in need, we fulfill the words of Christ. By following the Golden Rule in our attitude, behavior, and conduct, we make the world a better place and make our own lives better too. —**CONCLUSION**

You only love someone when you are willing to sacrifice for them; without sacrifice, there is no love. —**CONCLUSION**

From the Pages of *The Criminal: The Power of An Apology*

Failing at an early age produces character, determination, and humility, all of which can never be learned without it. If you do fail, however, it means you had the courage to take a risk, which is in itself, quite admirable **– CHAPTER 1**

Failing should be thought of like a photograph. You see it, but only for the instant in which the image was captured. Photography can be misleading, just like failing. **– CHAPTER 1**

Failing is not failure; how you react to your failure is the indication of whether you have truly failed or not. **– CHAPTER 1**

Courage often is a result of failure in the same way that success is a result of courage; therefore, to achieve success in life, you have to overcome failure with courage. **– CHAPTER 1**

The only way to be found is to admit we are lost. **– CHAPTER 2**

We all hope; it is what we hope for that demonstrates where our true heart is. All the criminal hoped for is to be found again; in his repentance and in his character, that happened. **– CHAPTER 2**

With Christianity, the less you are in control, the more you are in control. **– CHAPTER 2**

The nice thing about knowing that Jesus died for our sins is that once we know that simple truth, our lives are transformed. Sin in no longer chasing us; we know longer have to dodge and weave to hide: we are free, but only if we admit our sin. **– CHAPTER 2**

In making yourself vulnerable to the ones you love, a foundation as solid as a rock is formed. **– CHAPTER 2**

Admitting your blind spot is a challenging thing to, but it produces a realness is relationships, because it shows the person you know that you are only human. That humbleness opens the door for them to be humble back to you, opening the way for a deeper form of communication than you thought was possible. **– CHAPTER 2**

I often find myself trying to be perfect, and when I'm not, I find myself trying to cover up my sin when I should be doing the opposite because Christ died for me. **– CHAPTER 2**

The last thing I like to do is admit that I am wrong, but when I do, I know God is smiling; after all, it means my complete trust is in him. **– CHAPTER 2**

To God however, beauty means admitting we are broken and lost, needing to pick up God's rhythms to regain it. Whatever we do is not enough because we have all fallen short, so very short of his Glory. Only in the cross, can we regain that beauty. **– CHAPTER 2**

The opposite of sarcasm is vulnerability. You can tell when a man is strong when he is more attuned to the latter rather than the former. **– CHAPTER 3**

Without integrity, a person is empty. The emptiness comes from that person's lack of respect for reality; in life, reality accounts for everything that is worthwhile. **– CHAPTER 4**

To make a difference, we have to make a change. The reason for this is rather simple: we are all fallen—in need of his saving grace—
CHAPTER 4

It is only when we hide our sin that we get into trouble. Admitting your trouble is the surest way to get out of trouble in Christianity. **–**
CHAPTER 4

Being honest doesn't require you to be good-looking, smart, or clever, it only requires showing your authentic self to the world. Chances are, if you are honest, people will appreciate you more, listen to you more, and value you more. The reason for this is simple: you will now be set apart in a rare class. **– CHAPTER 4**

To take it learning even further, one has to learn from anybody and everybody, even the flawed. In doing so, your life will be changed, and once your life is changed, you will change others. **– CHAPTER 5**

Only when we admit that we are less, and He is more, will we be found. The reason for this simple: admitting that we are less doesn't make us *less*, it makes us *more*. **– CHAPTER 5**

With power, often comes pride. That pride is not from above, but down below. The only thing we need to be prideful of is what Jesus did for us on the cross. It was the opposite of prideful. Because of this, it was definition of powerful. – **CHAPTER 5**

Jesus never seeks earthly might. To be a king is to be rich, powerful, carry a good name, and have lots of servants. I guess Jesus never got the memo. For him, power was in being *with* us, not *over* us. – **CHAPTER 5**

Most people are too proud to learn, but the most impactful of people always take the position that in order to impact people, you can never learn enough. – **CHAPTER 5**

We're blessed in that when Jesus said, "It is finished", what it meant for us is that it was only getting started. Through his death on the cross, we could start to love again, start to matter again, but most of all, we could start to heal again. In healing again, we can start to live again. And we are doubly blessed in that most leaders close their doors. Most famous people try to avoid the paparazzi and fans. Not Jesus though. He told us he would be with us until the end of the age. – **CHAPTER 5**

We are all fake, all lost, void of anything worthwhile without the blood of Jesus. We all need blood in order to survive. Why live only to survive, why not live to thrive? We can, but only with the blood of Jesus. Only his blood is pure, that is for certain. – **CHAPTER 6**

When we repent, we are secure. It's a security that is much more comforting than a 401K or a seat-belt in a car. It's a security that transcends all understanding, and once you have it, all you want to do is pass it on. After all, to give that security is to give life. And it's not just life on this earth, it's life everlasting. – **CHAPTER 6**

I need Jesus' blood just as I need oxygen, food, water, and shelter. Without it, I can never survive, never thrive. Without it I am a nobody, I can achieve nothing. With it, I am not only powerful, I am free. – **CHAPTER 6**

We're often taught to present our best self to the world even though deep down we know this is not for the best. – **CHAPTER 6**

You can tell how much someone believes in the cross by how open they are about their own sin. – **CHAPTER 6**

Thankfulness shouldn't be situation-based because difficult times have a way of shaping us in a stronger, more effective way than a seemingly encouraging time. It's more challenging to grow when things are going well. When you're at the very bottom, upward is the only direction you can go. – **CHAPTER 6**

To be thankful isn't to walk around with a smile on your face all the time. Jesus didn't have a smile on his face when he was crucified. After all, didn't he cry out, "why have you forsaken me?" He did have the wherewithal to trust God during that time, however. When you trust in God during the toughest of times, He credits that as thankfulness. – **CHAPTER 8**

For me, gratitude can frame meaningless drudgery into meaningful opportunities."

Disciple is the root word of discipline. So why is discipline seen as an *extremely* negative word and disciple as an extremely *positive* word? **– CHAPTER 9**

It might seem like a paradox, but you want to try to be a person that no one wants to be around because when he leaves your presence they are immediately disappointed by the decreased level of character and encouragement they are now forced to be around in terms of dealing with other people. **– CHAPTER 9**

I challenge the people I respect, but to those who have neither the capacity nor ability to change, I am silent. **– CHAPTER 9**

The criminal serves as a guide to us all. He's humble, yet unafraid, clever, without the usual pretentiousness; but most of all, he is loyal, and in his loyalty, he became the first convert to Christianity; in doing so, he joined Jesus in paradise forever. **– CONCLUSION**

From the Pages of *He Spoke with Authority: Get, then Give the Advantage of Confidence*

It made me realize two things: to be happy for another person's success doesn't make you *less* of a person, it makes you *more* of a person. It also made me realize that the common perception that a true friend is one who is with you during the worst of times is wrong. A friend who is with you during the best of your times is truly there for you for he is not jealous, but happy for you, showing true love. - **CHAPTER 1**

All of us should have the utmost confidence in ourselves for one primary reason: what Jesus did for us on the cross. Once we realize that, indeed, we are made perfect by His actions, we can shake off all the insecurities that hold us back and start to live for Him. It's tough for us to comprehend this because we live in such a merit-based society; luckily for, our merit was earned by Jesus' blood on the cross. Nothing else can make us more whole or secure. – **CHAPTER 1**

People are going to doubt you if you possess the courage to do anything great. Let them do so: chances are they are jealous that you have the guts and talent to try. – **CHAPTER 1**

It's okay to think that you are capable of greatness. That's not a sin in God's eyes. Just make sure you are using your talents and so forth for God's glory, not just your own. The scariest scenario for the Devil is to have a confident God-fearing human carrying out the Lord's work. The Devil is not at all scared of insecure Christ followers; in fact, that's who he takes advantage of the most." –

CHAPTER 2

Don't let others lead you down your own path; let God do that; God knew you first. **– CHAPTER 2**

We can bring heaven here on earth, but only when we display confidence in ourselves. Sitting on the sidelines is futile. **– CHAPTER 2**

Do yourself a favor: let the force of confidence get you moving. When you do, you will move others and, in the process, be moved yourself. **– CHAPTER 2**

For parents to stifle their child's optimism is to not only stifle their own dreams, but the dreams of others. The reason for this is simple: once one achieves their own dreams, they often help others to achieve their own dreams; at least the great ones do. **– CHAPTER 2**

Protectors are able to protect us because the security they have in themselves; they refuse to be insecure because they know they have to be secure for others. **- CHAPTER 2**

The Bible tells us that to much has been given, much is expected; go into your day knowing that you have been entrusted with much and it is all for His glory, not just for your own pleasure. With this new way of thinking, you'll find that your pleasure becomes His glory. Ultimately, you know your faith is strong when you say "thank you" to God, and God says, "no, *thank you.*" This means that your purpose in life and His will are one in the same. **– CHAPTER 2**

There is nothing more noble than sticking up for someone else when they have been wronged. There is one characteristic that a human being must have to do this: confidence. Sticking up for yourself is easy, but to stick up for another human being shows a blend of both unselfishness and confidence which the mother and father of what Christianity is all about. – **CHAPTER 3**

You can't always be safe and confident at the same time. And chances are if you are too confident, you are doing something that is too safe. - **CHAPTER 3**

When you're the only one that can stick up for yourself, do so with courage and you may just find the respect of the people who have tried to trample you down. At the very least, they may find some empathy for the situation. – **CHAPTER 3**

Security in oneself leads to security in the other person. It shows that you are humble, not so much putting the weight of the world in yourself, but ultimately others. If you're secure with yourself, you'll find yourself reaching out to make sure other people are secure with themselves. In doing so, you'll become that much more secure with yourself. - **CHAPTER 3**

When you find yourself sticking up for people more and more, you know that you are growing more and more confident; the insecure, however, only stick up for themselves. – **CHAPTER 3**

Other's affliction should affect all of us, and when it does, you know you're confident in your own skin. - **CHAPTER 3**

While it is noble to turn the other cheek, when another person is hurting you so much to the point where you have trouble living, it is not only okay to stick up for yourself, but God wants you to do so; he wants you to be strong so you can do His work. – **CHAPTER 3**

Getting out of abusive relationships is hard, but necessary. When you're in an abusive relationship, it is impossible to carry out God's will the best you can because in the back of your mind you're filled with all the trauma of the abusive relationship. – **CHAPTER 3**

Whatever seems unlikely, improbable, even if something has never happened before, it can happen through God. Is it okay to be nervous knowing that you are chosen by God to do his work? Yes, but just know that by putting your confidence in Him, you will in turn be more confident, being able to accomplish anything for Him. – **CHAPTER 4**

Once we have confidence in Him, he gives us all the confidence we need to do His work. God wants you to be confident; He knows that without it, the mission he has set before us will never be accomplished. – **CHAPTER 4**

When we look out for others, our confidence shows in plain light and cannot be hidden. God gave us confidence so we could save others just as He saved us on the cross. Once this shift of perspective in your thinking happens, you will be bolder, thus changing more lives. – **CHAPTER 4**

Confidence is like centrifugal force; it is never ceasing, it always extends to the receiver and back to the giver. It doesn't just unlock doors, it tears them down off its hinges so it will be easier for the next person walk through; or, better yet, run through. – **CHAPTER 4**

Confident people often sacrifice themselves so that the rest of us cannot only live but live well; these people aren't so bad after all, for they lived as Jesus lived.; they sacrifice just as Jesus sacrificed.- **CHAPTER 4**

When you're vulnerable with someone, there is a connection that cannot be broken. In laying down all your cards, you'll discover that you have the winning hand. The reason you win is by allowing the other person to see you clearly for the first time—allowing them to assist you when you need assistance, cry with you when you feel you need comfort, and help you stand when you feel as if you cannot bear your own weight. – **CHAPTER 5**

To be vulnerable is to be real, and in that vulnerability, you are strong. - **CHAPTER 5**

Intimacy is like that tough conversation that you don't want to have: you dread it, during it you're scared and frightened, but afterwards you're telling yourself: I can't wait to come back for more. The next time though, you dread it less, thus enabling you to be even more intimate; once again; after you've experienced it, you come back for more. - **CHAPTER 5**

What does having a mentor say about somebody? Well, ultimately, it shows that they are both confident and humble—two words that rarely go together. It shows that you are humble enough to feel that you *need* to improve and confident enough that you *can* improve. - **CHAPTER 6**

Confidence leads to empathy because of the security you have in yourself. With that security, you can give it to others who need it. – **CHAPTER 6**

To be a strong Christian, you must emit a different type of electricity to others. It's a type of electricity that only comes from confidence. You'll often find that once you emit that electricity toward others, you will get just as much back. – **CHAPTER 7**

Real love is not silent; it speaks to us in a way we are not used to hearing; therefore, there is no way to mute it like we turn like we mute TV commercials. Real love is strong, bold, courageous, and confident; it teaches us to dare in its daringness. – **CHAPTER 8**

From the Pages of *When I See It: Belief in the Uncertainty*

Laughter dampens our woes in a way that it not only stops the pain, but gives a chance to learn from it, thus enabling us to be stronger the next time. **– CHAPTER 2**

Shift your reason for happiness based on *other's* happiness instead of your *own*, and you will be more fulfilled; I guarantee it. **– CHAPTER 2**

"When you're given something, you've got to pass it... pass it on, pass it around, or pass it backwards. Not to do so is not only unappreciative, but also an insult to God." **– CHAPTER 2**

It's not just that when one door closes, another opens, often times you'll that when your door opens, you'll get to have the opportunity to open that same door for others— creating an environment that never could have happened if that originally door hadn't been closed. Having a door closed only means God is going to present you with an opportunity to open more doors for others—and Him—in the future. **– CHAPTER 2**

We are often fearful of what we don't know because fear is often born out of ignorance; the worst part of this is that it can lead to quick judgment—most the time that judgment being wrong. **– CHAPTER 3**

How is it that fail to see people for who they really are more often than not? Is it pride, is it pain? Or insecurity? As human beings, we are all so different, but nonetheless so similar in the fact that we often succumb to the mistake of rushing judgment on one another, and even if we don't rush that judgment, we often make the mistake of judging one another on inconsequential aspects of our life instead of things that matter. **– CHAPTER 3**

The cover—or the outside—distracts us from seeing what's on the inside more often than not even though it contains no content—or, nothing to learn from. When people refer to what percentage of a book they've read, they often describe their progress in the number of pages read. They're telling you how much content they have gotten through; only then can they truly judge a book. Judge people in the same way. Count the pages you've read before you start drawing conclusions. **– CHAPTER 3**

Layers in a cake can be challenging to read because if you look from the top down, you can't see that there are even layers in the first place; it just seems like there is one consistency in whatever it is you're looking at. But it you see the cake at eye level, you'll soon see a cake for what it's really worth—the whole picture. To see the whole picture, you must be at eye-level, meaning that you're willing to look at the cake in the same way it glances back at you. In the same way, humans must look at each other in the eye; they must make eye contact. Only then can you see the other person in their true light. **– CHAPTER 3**

It's difficult to realize that God is in control, but when we do, we have a better avenue to live out His will because deep down we always know that He wants what's best for us. During the moment this type of thinking can be challenging to say the least. People often say that patience is a virtue; what it is as well is a test—a test of your faith in God. **– CHAPTER 5**

Entrepreneurs who make a lot of money are so successful because they are able to think outside of the box. Thinking outside the box means the perimeter is going to bigger than simply thinking inside the box. It's a risk, and it ultimately takes more effort, but in the end, it's the only way to achieve success. When you think outside the box, and don't judge a book by its cover, paradoxically, you are able to within a person; you're able to see them for who they truly are. **– CHAPTER 7**

Beauty is found from within because our actions are ultimately the only thing we have control over. That's the gift of free-will. The cross is the most important thing in Christianity, but once your sins are atoned for, God doesn't want you just to pray all day and sing and thank Him for it, he wants you to be a man after His own heart and spread the Gospel. He wants you to do all these things in response to that great gift you were given. **– CHAPTER 7**

It's interesting how unselfishness acts often pay dividends for us in the future; it's almost as if God sees where our heart is, appreciates it, and rewards us for our self-denial. **– CHAPTER 6**

In the same vein, it's an interesting point to wander why God made us in the first place. An answer you might normally get to that question is that He was lonely; but that isn't it. Since God is all powerful, omnipotent, and perfect, he doesn't *need* anything. It's the same choice married parents make when they decide to have children: they do so out of love—an unselfish love that transcends all understanding. Not only did our God come down from heaven to atone for our sins, but he also created us in the first place and allows us to have a relationship with Him. **– CHAPTER 6**

A day spent without encouraging others is a day wasted; people need you to be that agent of God in their life; there is no greater impact on your life than to impact others. **– CHAPTER 6**

Walking with God also means that you are willing to take a risk; sometimes that risk may involve you may look like a complete fool to others. If that's the case don't sweat it, for a fool to humans is often just the person God uses most to carry out His will. **– CHAPTER 4**

It's interesting for me to look back on my own life and realize what has happened because certain things didn't happen. It reiterates to me that God had a plan for my life, and He knows not only how to shape it but direct it. **– CHAPTER 4**

When we hesitate, we are telling the thing or someone that we want that we don't want them—that they're not important in our life. When we have a chance to do God's will and don't act on it, we are telling Him that he is not the number one priority in our life. This disappoints God more than anything, because ultimately, he knows what's best for us. **– CHAPTER 4**

It was time to go into the world and see where I could leave my mark. My depression had ended now that I had finally seen some light, but what was I to do with my light? When you're an occasional runner, tying your shoes to go out and run is the hardest part; for me, it was time to tie my shoes. Learning how to tie one's shoes is something we learn how to do as a child, but the more and more we live, often times, the more and more we forget how to do this simple act. We're scared of what might happen if we fail; or, are we more afraid of what will happen if we succeed? Whatever it is, tying one's shoes is difficult, but with the Lord's help—and with His purpose in mind—we can do it each and every day. **– CHAPTER 4**

Compromising yourself is easy in times of trouble, but ultimately, there's always only one side that's right in disagreement, and that side is truth; to live the truth might mean sacrificing something, but in sacrificing that something, you'll find that you gain true honor and dignity—which could have never come without the sacrifice – **CHAPTER 3**

To start a relationship—whether it be romantic or simply friendship—there has to be a sense of permanence that will always be there. Without that, relationships cannot form properly—or at all. **– CHAPTER 6**

From the Pages of *Listen Up: Seek Enough Advice and One Day You'll Be Giving It*

Too often, we are too arrogant to know that we have much to learn in this world. Too often, we assume that we have a grasp on things, when in actuality, we have no clue what is going on. **– CHAPTER 1**

Why is listening and receiving advice so hard for many of us? It is as if we feel insulted when we receive help or are forced to listen. It is one thing to listen advice from someone who is older than us, but to listen to advice from someone who are own age or younger than us seems unfathomable. Oftentimes, the best of us feel humble enough to receive advice and listen, improving with every encounter. **– CHAPTER 1**

Truly being open to guidance doesn't mean that you don't know the answer, it means you are humble enough to admit that there's a possibility, as slight as it could be, that you don't know the answer. Having that type of mentality is the only way to grow, because you only grow when you are tested, and you in order to pass a test, you must listen. **- CHAPTER 1**

You never do know when you might receive a lesson from someone you deem less educated than you however high and mighty you think you are, so rather than close your ears, keep them open and you just might find that you'll advance. Call it wild, but you just might advance behind your wildest dreams. **– CHAPTER 1**

To understand someone, you've got to listen; you've got to be paying close attention to what the other is going through more than what you are going through. Environmentalists often says tread lightly and leave no trace. Understanding someone can be phrased in the opposite manner: tread heavily where they have tread, then you'll be able to make a trace on their hearts & in their lives. - **CHAPTER 2**

Being skilled will take you far, but if you get to the point where you are so skilled that you don't believe you can need aid to better yourself, you are in treacherous territory. - **CHAPTER 3**

Whether we'd like to admit it or not, we're drawn to people who listen to us. Usually the people who listen to us tend to be in a lower or similar status than us. That's why, when someone we perceive as powerful than us takes the time an effort to listen to us, we appreciate that instance more than a normal instance. God, in his mighty power, never fails to listen to us. If God never fails to listen to us, why do we constantly fail to listen to others? – **CHAPTER 3**

I realize many of my writing is of a very personal tone, especially on the subject of my fight with mental illness, but when I realized that my writing was having an impact on people in a positive way, all the embarrassment and shame went away… God gave me the ability to think, be creative, and write in order to help people whether they be Christian or not. I take great pride in being part of God's team, and it only happened because I listened to his call. – **CHAPTER 4**

Listening can be oh so difficult because of our pride. We like to think that we know it all, more often than not, and to receive advice is seen as something weak, lacking true purpose. **– CHAPTER 4**

Our Lord our God tells us to live boldly, to take a risk, to surprise many including ourselves. How does one gain the capacity to surprise oneself? I've learned, that more often than not, in order to have the capacity to surprise ourselves, we must look at life as someone who is at the bottom of a swimming pool. No matter how hard we try to stay at the bottom, we seem to always come up with force. Trusting that God gave you the force to do anything seems incomprehensible is something that must always been implanted in the back of your mind. **– CHAPTER 5**

 A stud's purpose is to form a vertical structural load. It can also be non load-bearing. Studs hold in place windows, doors, interior finish, exterior sheathing or siding, insulation and utilities, but, if you ask a contractor, what the most important thing a stud does is to give shape to a building. Finding a person who shapes you is the person who God wants you to be with. **– CHAPTER 6**

To be truly known by the other starts with the other listening and absorbing information to realize not only what other makes the person tick, but what moves the other person—what makes the other person not only get out of bed, but also keeps the person from going back to bed in the middle of the day. **– CHAPTER 6**

Gardeners and contractors may not seem like they would at all be a similar profession, but they are both building something—something that is meant to last and be used. Both professions also require listening. Not listening in the sense of hearing but listening in the sense of knowing what their admirers or habitants want. If they're good at they're profession, their wants begin to be innate; they naturally want to build a foundation that lasts until eternity. – **CHAPTER 6**

When you think of a leader who is adaptable, you think of someone who is not only calm under pressure, but someone who is not naïve to different circumstances; they can assure their followers that no matter what, their plan will work whatever is thrown their way. – **CHAPTER 7**

When people think of arrogance, they often judge someone based on the fact if this person brags a lot. I, on the other hand, look to see if they are humble enough to admit that they in fact do not know it all. – **CHAPTER 7**

Luckily, with God's word, we have instructions on how to make every decision in life. All we have to do is listen to him and trust that even if it is the harder path, listening to his choice makes us live with purpose. – **CHAPTER 8**

I've sometimes wondered why I use so many quotations in my books from others, and, at the beginning of my books have included two or three from each chapter. I've come to the conclusion it is because, above all, people tell us quotes and share quotes with us to encourage, to inspire. – **CHAPTER 9**

Find people that challenge you. When you do this, you'll often find the challenges you face in the future are less difficult because the training this person has put you through. The weak surround themselves with people who are too timid to stick up to them, while the strong get the feeling that no future battle should be left untested.

– CHAPTER 9

By admitting that I was not only wrong in one area of my actions but could have improved my area in another area actions, I just got a lot better. If we think about it, when someone critiques our actions, instead of our first thought being to say that they're wrong, we might ask them for additional things we need to work on because we might feel as if they are tip-toeing around us to make sure our feelings hurt if they brought up additional issues. – **CHAPTER 9**

Leaders are on the unquenchable quest to get better. The best CEO's make performance reviews twosided instead of the boss just focusing on the employee is performing. This way, the CEO gets better, and when the CEO gets better, he/she can lead more effectively. – **CHAPTER 9**

Music has a way of lifting us up in a way that nothing else quite can. It moves us, challenges us; in short, it is the both the glue and motor that binds and pushes us to pursue life in a different way we never thought was possible. We listen to music; not only to hear the instruments, but to hear the lyrics teach just as a school-teacher lectures at a podium. Will we listen to them? Are we both humble and strong enough to do just that? – **CHAPTER 10**

Age is not only the exact prerequisite for wisdom, but experience. A young person can draw from experiences just as an elder can. It doesn't happen very often, but when it does, you better being willing to listen and be humble, for one of the definitions of humble is ranking low in a hierarchy or scale. Can you make yourself low to become high? – **CHAPTER 10**

My best contributions to the world have started with listening, while my failures have often been the direct result of an ability to listen. – **CHAPTER 11**

The strong don't mind feeling as if they don't have to be in control. Control to them means controlling themselves first. From there, they feel like they have a handle on every situation that arises. – **CHAPTER 12**

Our eyes swell when are filled with emotion. The only way that can happen to us is if we feel listened to. When are listened to, feel that we are cared for, and, when we are cared for, we know are loved. – **CHAPTER 12**

You feel a void most in your life not when you cannot have the latest dress, car, or house, but when you lose something that is dear to you. This is why relationships are so much more important than things. – **CHAPTER 12**

When you receive and or give meaningful advice, a bond is formed between both individuals that can't be broken. It's as if you become on the same teams, one hand lifting up the other towards a common goal. – **CHAPTER 12**

From the Pages of *Alone at the Lunch Table: How to Rise from Rejection*

You're not accepted until you are rejected. **– CHAPTER 1**

All of us in our own lives face times where we can or cannot earn admission into an institution, get the job we want to get, or be in the relationship we want to be in. If you do get denied, we have no authority to be angry, or depressed because of one reason: we don't know what is best for us; only God knows that. **– CHAPTER 1**

Sometimes, when God tells you no, he is really telling you yes, for a no to you now might mean a yes to you later on. It all depends on the work God has in store for you. Sometimes, what seems like a defeat is really just the start—the start of something great. **– CHAPTER 2**

How awesome is it that God trusts us to do His work and doesn't do it alone? When you delegate, you uplift; when you feel as though you are the only person skilled enough to do the task and don't ask for help, you discourage. When the game is tied in the 9th inning, everyone wants to be the person the coach calls on to pinch-hit for the pitcher and get the job done. God could do it himself, easily, but he knows everyone wants a challenge, which gives you an opportunity to shine. With Jesus' blood, we already shine, but God wants our life to have purpose. Delegating leads to others shining, which leads to purpose. Life throws curveballs at us all the time, but if your purpose is His will, you'll break that tie. **– CHAPTER 2**

Detaching yourself from the situation and looking at things from an objective instead of a subjective point of view is the first step to getting over your rejection. **– CHAPTER 3**

I often takes things personally when I don't get a job I wanted. This again, forces me to step backward instead of going forward. It sounds cliché, but whatever that thing you didn't get was not meant for you in the first place; it turns out that it wouldn't advance His kingdom. It's easier said than done but detach immediately after rejection and you'll find that it is much easier to deal with. **– CHAPTER 3**

Often times, when get rejected, we think we are being put down, when in actuality, as a result of the rejection, we could be lifted higher. **– CHAPTER 3**

Have you thought about something in your own life that you *must* have? One must make sure that what *you* want aligns with what God wants. The Devil is very clever. Wanting what seems to be a Godly thing can often become worshipping an idol. **– CHAPTER 4**

How do you start winning more arguments? I'll give you this one tip: when you find yourself losing an argument, the faster you denounce your stance and admit you're wrong, the more arguments you will win in the future. The reason for this is your thinking will be sharper and you won't find yourself making the same mistake or succumbing to the same fallacy in a future argument. **– CHAPTER 4**

Aggression, in combination with a deft touch, has served many a leader well. One could say Jesus, the ultimate leader, possessed both in abundance. – **CHAPTER 4**

For the commoner, they believe that people want something they can't have. This technically is true. What I've found over the past few years though, however, is that playing hard to get rarely works out in the end. – **CHAPTER 5**

The biggest challenge we face as humans is the challenge to dare to be different. – **CHAPTER 6**

When we pick up the phone and call someone, ultimately, we don't know if they are going to pick up on the other end. Still, in my opinion, it's worth making that call and reaching out because you never know if that person will help you reach your dreams. – **CHAPTER 6**

When you want something that another person has, show the other person you want it and more often than not, it will become yours. Sounds pretty simple, but in our world of email, text message, and social media, it is not. – **CHAPTER 6**

Be careful when you look down on someone, thinking that they are behind you. I've found that people who appear in your rearview mirror can enter your blind spot sooner than you think, and, while you can't see them anymore and think that they now in your blind spot, you'll be remiss to realizing that the positions have switched; you're now in *their* blind spot because they're ahead of you. They'll stay ahead of you because, unlike you, they're not looking down on anyone and are instead, zooming ahead. – **CHAPTER 6**

From The Pages of *After the Shampoo: Conditioned For Excellence*

"Your parents are important. They are literally the first people that condition your future behavior." – **CHAPTER 1**

"The absolute worst thing that can happen in life is to be conditioned by someone who is good or great—incorrectly thinking in the back of your mind the whole time that they were excellent." – **CHAPTER 1**

"When I think of the most ingrateful people in my life, I think of people who feel like they *deserve* everything." – **CHAPTER 1**

"The most arrogant people I have met in my life aren't the ones who didn't brag about themselves, they are the ones who were unwilling to listen and unwilling to apologize." – **CHAPTER 2**

"The most successful people in life leverage off other people's success instead of being jealous of them, knowing full well that the momentum of that other's success will lead to them their own success." – **CHAPTER 2**

"Never let someone else's success become your own defeat." – **CHAPTER 2**

"You see, the more attention we get in life, when that attention gets directed towards someone else, our first reaction is naturally to feel jealous. If this happens to you, don't beat yourself up about it, but you realize that you must turn that jealousy into encouragement. This way it's a win-win situation for both sides." – **CHAPTER 2**

"In physics, a lever amplifies an input force to provide a greater output force, which is said to provide *leverage*. The ratio of the output force to the input force is the mechanical advantage of the lever. The *mechanical advantage* of a lever is the ratio of the load the lever overcomes and the effort a person or system applies to the lever to overcome some load or resistance. In simple words and as per the formula, it's the ratio of load and effort. Are you going to let the other person's success push you *forward* or push you *back*?" — **CHAPTER 2**

"How do you know if someone has made a big impact on this earth? The easiest way to see if this has happened is if someone says a person—who never said the quote in the first place—said that quote." – **CHAPTER 3**

"There's a reason why people have misattributed these quotes to these people: they are more famous than the person who originally said it, thus making it more powerful of a quote." – **CHAPTER 3**

"Throughout this book, I encourage you, the reader, to be conditioned by not good, not great, but excellent role models. I've got a question for you, though: how much more can you grow as person and in your walk with God if you can take the advice of people you don't like or don't respect? True, they might not have as good of as advice as the excellent, but you still might be able to grow from them." – **CHAPTER 3**

"When giving advice, keep in mind that what you are about to propose to the other person is something new, something foreign. When you give someone a new food to try, you don't give them a whole spoonful, but only a bite. This is the way you should go about giving advice." – **CHAPTER 3**

"The old can teach the young and the young can teach the old." – **CHAPTER 3**

"All of us, no matter how successful we become, need encouragement." – **CHAPTER 3**

"To condition someone, you must both challenge and encourage at an equal rate. When one gets in front of the other, excellence never happens." – **CHAPTER 3**

"Oftentimes we cannot know God's ways; we can not see them. But, we have to always keep in mind that he can see us. It must be this way in order for Him to condition us, which in turn brings us along." – **CHAPTER 3**

"As human beings, we are naturally conditioned to seek the approval of fellow man. All of us like to fit in, but at the same time, all of seek to be excellent. I've noticed that to be excellent, you have to sacrifice your incessant desire to fit in." – **CHAPTER 4**

"As Williamson says, liberate yourself from your own fear. When you do so, others will follow suit. You will raise the bar for all. Excellence has a way of causing more excellence in the same way a virus spreads; it can truly be exponential." – **CHAPTER 4**

"Dare to be the first one to do something; in doing so, you'll surprise many maybe even yourself. If you do something that has already been done before, the chances of you being remembered by ages to come go down significantly. If you're not consistently pushing yourself to be the first, you may as well not even attempt what you are doing, for it is in vain." – **CHAPTER 4**

When someone above you, with more experience and wisdom than you encourages you it is impossible to forget it; we're conditioned to not be taken seriously. – **CHAPTER 4**

Often times, when I think of my relationship with God, when he causes something to happen or not happen in my life, I realize that he has complete control of it—much more control of it then I have … Because of this, he is able to bring me along. – **CHAPTER 5**

To this day, the success I have had in writing, my technology sales career, and the education reform that I am working on currently, is due to the fact that I am not afraid to get people's opinion on matters. I'm constantly asking for advice; that's what my 6th book is about: being humble enough to seek advice. When you do this, you can become a subject matter expert on any topic even if you don't technically have a PhD in it. – **CHAPTER 5**

To become excellent, you must remember that if someone is critiquing you they think you are capable of something special—something to be remembered. Usually, when we don't hear criticism, we are happy; it I as if we did nothing wrong; I encourage us to do the opposite: we must seek out criticism in order to keep getting better. When you don't hear any, rather than be delighted, have the wherewithal to think that someone might not be taking you seriously. – **CHAPTER 5**

True, our present and future actions are dictated by our past actions, but at the same time, we have free will—we have the choice in which our destiny will be shaped. – **CHAPTER 5**

To be truly excellent, we must not be afraid to decline certain things, even if that thing be our very life. – **CHAPTER 5**

In order to influence, we must be influenced first. – **CHAPTER 5**

Dreaming is necessary when you're an underdog, and because you're forced to dream, versus knowing you'll achieve success all along, you're forced to outwork your competition, thus enabling to you achieve that long-awaited dream. People often forget this when analyzing the data on whether one will succeed or not. – **CHAPTER 5**

Like I said before, to achieve your dreams, you need someone to help condition you; you need someone to help bring you along. – **CHAPTER 5**

In the most meaningful relationships, each party must be humble enough to accept help from the other party. Without this, the type of learning and improved that is needed to become excellent can never happen. – **CHAPTER 6**

When you think outside the box, it not only levels the playing field for you an your competitors, it might even give you an edge to beat them. Because you're competition has more talent than you to begin with, they've never been forced to think outside the box; they've never been forced to be creative. If you remember this, you might just become like David and beat Goliath. – **CHAPTER 7**

As an underdog, if you already know what the person who is highly favored is going to do, use that to your advantage. As the cliché says, "knowledge is power." If you already know what there move is going to be, you have the power then to make your move. Battle is like chess; it's how you respond and react, can you be bold enough to make the right move? – **CHAPTER 7**

We must get outside of ourselves if we ever want to make anything of ourselves. When we look deeper into what I just said, we can discover the reason for this. A synonym for outside is exterior. When we think of the exterior of a peanut butter sandwich that is given to a child, he/she often doesn't want to eat the crust, but our parents growing up demanded that we finish our plate. One of the ten commandments from Exodus is "Honor your father and your mother, that your days may be long upon the land which the Lord your God is giving you." Ultimately, Jamal honors his mother and himself by go to the new school. When we honor our parents and "finish our plate," we can start to get outside and challenge ourselves more and more each and every day. – **CHAPTER 7**

For any leader to be successful, you have to not only have energy, but provide it to others in abundance. One way to do that, believe it or not, is to deflect attention and praise away from yourself. This, in turn, puts the emphasis back on the people, challenging them to do the impossible. – **CHAPTER 7**

Today, we see politicians puff themselves up, trying to be the Savior that we don't need. We need someone with humble audacity, not someone with puffed up arrogance. If we can get a candidate to the former, we might just have ourselves the next Washington. – **CHAPTER 7**

So many of us make excuses for why things haven't gone the way they have when it actuality, things could have gone much differently for us had we seized opportunities along the way. To seize an opportunity, it's not intelligence that matters the most, but vision. Once your vison becomes reality, you can start to notice that the things holding you back no propel you onward. **– CHAPTER 7**

To get back on your feet after calamity has struck is not easy. But remember, with daringness comes determination, and with determination comes the possibility of the pursuit of excellence. With unthinking sureness, what was once a possibility can become fulfilled. But this can only happen if you take the chance to begin with. **– CHAPTER 7**

Marriage is a *big* deal to God—being in a dating relationship or being engaged, not so much. Never find yourself saying to yourself, "well, if I had only been single, I might have ended up with that right person God had in store for me." **– CHAPTER 8**

All of these passages or verses have one thing in common: all encourage you to judge your fellow man. In today's society, what Christians often do is the direct *opposite* of what God wants you to do: people often talk negatively behind others back, but don't confront the person directly. In doing so, they do judge the other person, but don't make the other person better. **– CHAPTER 8**

To better your fellow man by pointing out a flaw that they are doing is not only not a sin, it is necessary for them to become closer to God and more Christlike. Hebrews 12:1 says, "whoever loves discipline loves knowledge, but he who hates correction is stupid."

Our first instinct is to feel stupid and less than perfect when someone corrects us, but when we get to the point when we understand that they are doing so to better our relationship with The Lord, we know we are getting to the place where He wants us to be, which is admitting that we have never arrived. – **CHAPTER 8**

When you think deeply about something, realizing why certain people take certain actions or act a certain way, you come to the conclusion that above all, people will respond to incentives. – **CHAPTER 8**

APPENDIX A
COMPLETE LIST OF TIGER WOODS' INJURIES

December 1994: Surgery on left knee to remove two benign tumors and scar tissue.

Dec. 13, 2002: Surgery on left knee to remove fluid inside and outside the ACL and remove benign cysts from his left knee. Misses the season opener in 2003.

August 2007: Ruptures the ACL in his left knee while running on a golf course after the British Open, but is able to keep playing. Wins five of the last six tournaments he plays, including the PGA Championship for his 13th major.

April 15, 2008: Two days after the Masters, has arthroscopic surgery on his left knee to repair cartilage damage.

May 2008: Advised weeks before the U.S. Open that he has two stress fractures of the left tibia and should rest for six weeks, the first three weeks on crutches.

June 24, 2008: Eight days after winning the U.S. Open, has surgery to repair the ACL in his left knee by using a tendon from his right thigh. Additional cartilage damage is repaired. Misses the rest of the season and does not return until the Match Play Championship at the end of February 2009.

December 2008: Injured his Achilles tendon in his right leg as he was running while preparing to return to golf.

Nov. 27, 2009: Hospitalized overnight with a sore neck and a cut lip that required five stitches when the SUV he was driving ran over a fire hydrant and into a tree.

May 9, 2010: Withdrew from the final round of The Players Championship, citing a bulging disk. He later said it was a neck issue that caused tingling in his right side, and that it first became a problem as he began practicing harder for his return to the Masters a month earlier.

April 10, 2011: Injures his left Achilles tendon hitting from an awkward stance below Eisenhower's Tree on the 17th at Augusta National. Withdraws from the Wells Fargo Championship.

May 12, 2011: Withdraws from The Players Championship after a 42 on the front nine. Diagnosed with an MCL sprain in his left knee and in his left Achilles tendon. He misses the next two months, including two majors, returning at the Bridgestone Invitational.

March 11, 2012: Feels tightness in his left Achilles tendon and withdraws after 11 holes of the final round in the Cadillac Championship at Doral. He wins in his next start at Bay Hill, his first PGA Tour victory since the scandal in his personal life.

Aug. 24, 2012: Moves stiffly during the second round of The Barclays and later says he felt pain in his lower back, which he attributed to a soft mattress in his hotel room.

June 13, 2013: Is seen shaking his left arm during the opening round of the U.S. Open. He later says it's a left elbow strain that he injured while winning The Players Championship a month earlier. He misses two tournaments and returns at the British Open.

Aug. 11, 2013: Said he felt tightness in his back during the final round of the PGA Championship.

Aug. 21, 2013: Two weeks after the PGA Championship, he only chips and putts on the back nine of the pro-am at The Barclays, complaining of a stiff neck and back that he attributed to a soft bed in the hotel. By Sunday at The Barclays, he dropped to his knees after one shot because of back spasms.

March 2, 2014: Withdraws after 13 holes of the final round at The Honda Classic because of lower back pain and spams, describing it as similar to what he felt at The Barclays.

March 9, 2014: Plays the final 12 holes with pain in his lower back, saying it began to flare up after hitting out of the bunker from an awkward lie in the Cadillac Championship at Doral. He shoots 78, the highest score of his career in a final round.

March 19, 2014: Withdraws from the Arnold Palmer Invitational because of the persistent pain in his back. He was the two-time defending champion.

March 31, 2014: Has surgery in Utah for a pinched nerve.

April 1, 2014: Announced he will miss the Masters and not return to golf until the summer.

Sept. 18, 2015: Underwent a second micro-discectomy surgery two days earlier to remove a disc fragment that was pinching his nerve.

October 2015: Woods has a procedure to "relieve discomfort" in his back and sets no timetable for his return to the PGA Tour.

April 20, 2017: Woods undergoes a fourth back surgery. The spinal fusion, labeled "a success" was to alleviate pain he had been experiencing in his back and leg.

March 4, 2019: Woods withdraws from the Arnold Palmer Invitational with a neck strain

Source: https://www.pga.com/archive/news/pga-tour/complete-list-tiger-woods-injuriesPublished on Tuesday, March 5, 2019. Retrieved 5/22/2011.

APPENDIX B

Boyd, Delainey <<u>Delainey.Boyd@mail.house.gov</u>>
Fri 1/15/2021 3:16 PM

To: Thomas Fellows

Hi Thomas,

Can we do 10am CST on the 3rd of February? And no need to pull together policy, I'll be happy to hear your ideas as a next step, no need to do special prep.

Best,

Delainey Boyd
Scheduler
Congresswoman Lizzie Fletcher (TX-07)
119 Cannon House Office Building
Washington, D.C. 20515
(202) 225-2571

<u>View the COVID-19 Community Resource Guide</u>
PLEASE NOTE: *Any meetings with Congresswoman Lizzie Fletcher are scheduled pending the House schedule. If a last minute schedule change occurs, the meeting will be handled by her staff. Thank you in advance for your cooperation and understanding!*